JOHN AND THE JESUS BOAT

Episode One

AD 27 – On the Road

Rolin Bruno

Copyright © 2018 by Rolin Bruno.

Cover credits to: Yigal Allon Center, Ginosar, Israel, and the Israel Antiquities Authority

Episode number one in the series, John and the Jesus Boat

Originally published as JOHN!, Library of Congress 2017901155.

All rights reserved. No part of this book may be used or reproduced by any means, graphic, electronic, or mechanical, including photocopying, recording, taping, or by any information storage retrieval system without the written permission of the author except in the case of brief quotations within critical articles or reviews.

Scripture quotations taken from the New American Standard Bible, Copyright 1960, 1962, 1963, 1968, 1971, 1972, 1973, 1975, 1977, 1995 by The Lockman Foundation. Used by permission. (www.Lockman.org)

Scripture taken from the Holy Bible, NEW INTERNATIONAL VERSION. Copyright 1973, 1978, 1984, 2011 by Biblica, Inc. All rights reserved worldwide. Used by permission.

NEW INTERNATIONAL VERSION and NIV are registered trademarks of Biblica, Inca. Use of either trademark for the offering of goods or services requires the prior written consent of Biblica US, Inc.

Scripture quotations taken from The Holy Bible, English Standard Version (ESV), copyright 2001 by Crossway, a publishing ministry of Good News Publishers. Used by permission. All rights reserved.

Scripture taken from Good News Translation (Today's English Version, Second Edition) copyright 1992 American Bible Society.

Scripture quotations taken from the Holy Bible, New Living Translation, copyright 1996, 2004. Used by permission of Tyndale House Publishers, Inc., Wheaton Illinois 60189. All rights reserved.

Printed in the United States of America

ISBN: 978-1-949362-25-1 (Paperback)
ISBN: 978-1-949362-24-4 (eBook)

Library of Congress Control Number: 2018952095

STONEWALL PRESS
PAVING YOUR WAY TO SUCCESS

Stonewall Press
363 Paladium Court
Owings Mills, MD 21117
www.stonewallpress.com
1-888-334-0980

The Jesus Boat

The cover image includes an ancient fishing boat from the first century that may have been used by Simon Peter the Apostle. It was discovered in 1986 on the north-west shore of the Sea of Galilee near ancient Capernaum.

The remains of the boat are 27 feet long and over 7 feet wide. Built mainly of cedar planks, the boat had a shallow draft with a flat bottom, allowing it to get close to shore for fishing. Four rowing positions allowed the boat to be propelled using a five-man crew. With its mast and tiller, wind power could be used to propel the boat. Separately, a tile mosaic from the first century was discovered that depicts what these boats looked like.

The wood for the boat was harvested between 120 BC and AD 40, based on radio-carbon dating. Nails and pottery including a cooking pot and lamp were found near the boat, and the hull was constructed with "mortise and tenon" technology, all of which set a final date for the boat between 50 BC and AD 50.

This ancient Sea of Galilee boat is an example of the type of craft used in the first century for both fishing and transportation across the lake. Jesus' earliest disciples were professional fishers who used boats like this. These boats were important to Jesus' ministry, and are mentioned 40 times in the Gospels. There is no evidence connecting this particular boat to Jesus or his disciples.

You can view this first century boat for yourself: It is on display near the Sea of Galilee in the Yigal Allon museum in Ginosar, Israel.

About the Author

Rolin Bruno is a Bible scholar and street evangelist with a vivid imagination that fills the gaps in Bible stories.

He has served as pastor at a storefront church on Skid Row in Los Angeles and as a street evangelist in the cities of Southern California, Western Pennsylvania, and the Gulf Coast of Mississippi.

Rolin has a calling to serve the homeless. In Louisiana and Mississippi, he served as a home missionary to stricken residents after the devastation of Hurricane Katrina, teaching spiritual disciplines and twelve-step recovery from addictions. In Pennsylvania, he served as a street evangelist to pre-teen street kids, and helped lead them through the Youth Alpha program to answer their questions about God and Jesus.

Rolin is a 2003 BA graduate of Vanguard University of Southern California, studying religion and ministry. He continued at Vanguard to earn a Master's degree in religion and Bible. His 2006 master's thesis is on the letter of Jude, "Jude and the Scoffers." This 278-page opus is available for purchase at http://www.tren.com.

He is an ordained deacon of the Communion of Evangelical Episcopal Churches and of the Anglican Communion in North America, and has a heart for planting new Celebrate Recovery chapters.

Rolin lives in the mountains of Southern California and is an avid camper and backpacker. He has hiked the Grand Canyon, Mount Whitney, the Inyo Mountains, and 570 miles of the Pacific Crest Trail.

Contents

About the Boat iii
About the Author v
Prologue: The Squall xi
    Tuesday, 14 January AD 27, 3:00 am

1 At the Back Gate 1
    Friday, 28 February AD 27, 10:00 am

2 At the Altar 11
    Saturday, 1 March AD 27, 7:00 am

3 A Voice Cries Out 19
    Wednesday, 5 March AD 27, 8:00 am

4 Pharisees and Sadducees 29
    Thursday, 6 March AD 27, 8:00 am

5 Samaritans and Soldiers 33
    Friday, 7 March AD 27, 8:00 am

6 Nathanael Returns 37
    Friday, 14 March AD 27, 8:00 am

7 Priests and Levites 43
    Sunday, 16 March AD 27, 7:00 am

8 The Lamb of God 49
    Monday, 17 March AD 27, 7:00 am

9 Meeting Jesus 51
    Tuesday, 18 March AD 27, 10:00 am

10 Hit the Road 55
Wednesday, 19 March AD 27, 6:00 am

11 A Wedding at Cana 57
Friday, 21 March AD 27, 11:00 am

12 Early Morning with Jesus 63
Saturday, 22 March AD 27, 6:00 am

13 Capernaum and Family 71
Sunday, 23 March AD 27, 5:00 pm

14 A Walk on the Beach 75
Thursday, 27 March AD 27, 9:00 am

15 City of David 79
Thursday, 3 April AD 27, 12:00 noon

16 A Talk with the Rabbi 83
Saturday, 5 April AD 27, 7:00 am

17 Lambs Aplenty 87
Wednesday, 9 April AD 27, 12:00 noon

18 Turning the Tables 91
Thursday, 10 April AD 27, 9:00 am

19 Passover Feast 93
Friday, 11 April AD 27, 6:00 am

20 Nicodemus at Night 97
Saturday, 12 April AD 27, 8:00 am

21 On the Road Again 101
Sunday, 13 April AD 27, 10:00 am

22 Baptizing in Judea 103
Monday, 14 April AD 27, 7:00 am

23 Bad News 107
Thursday, 29 May AD 27, 2:00 pm

24 Woman at the Well 109
    Monday, 2 June AD 27, 12:00 noon

25 Back in Galilee 113
    Saturday, 7 June AD 27, 9:00 am

26 Leaving Home.. 117
    Tuesday, 10 June AD 27, 4:00 pm

27 Nazareth Rejection 121
    Saturday, 14 June AD 27, 8:00 am

28 What's Wrong with Mom?..................................... 125
    Monday, 16 June AD 27, 3:00 pm

29 Mayor on a Horse.. 129
    Tuesday, 17 June AD 27, 8:00 am

30 Catching Fish 131
    Thursday, 26 June AD 27, 1:00 am

31 A Foul Spirit.. 135
    Friday, 27 June AD 27, 4:00 pm

32 Hidden Demons.. 139
    Saturday, 28 June AD 27, 6:00 pm

33 The Ears of Chorazin 141
    Monday, 30 June AD 27, 4:00 am

34 The Ears of Bethsaida.. 145
    Monday, 7 July AD 27, 12:00 noon

35 End of the Tour 147
    Tuesday, 30 September AD 27, 12:00 noon

36 A Leper in Judea 151
    Saturday, 11 October AD 29, 8:00 am

37 Hole in the Roof.. 153
    Tuesday, 28 October AD 27, 7:00 am

38 The Call of Matthew 155
    Thursday, 30 October AD 27, 9:00 am

39 What, No Fasting? 157
    Wednesday, 31 December AD 27, 10:00 am

Epilogue: The Son of God? 159
    Wednesday, 31 December AD 27, 8:00 pm

Notes and Suggested Bible Readings 161

Prologue

The Squall

Tuesday, 14 January AD 27, 3:00 am

"We're sinking! We're going to drown!"

"John, just keep bailing, and keep us headed to shore!" Andrew was terse as he and Philip strained at the oars—burly Andrew on the right, skinny Philip on the left. At just 16, Andrew fancied himself the master sailor, while John at the tiller, not quite 14, was still a bit unsure.

Philip said, "This is stupid! Why did I let you talk me into this?" He anxiously watched the waves from the sudden squall wash over the sides of the boat. This 27-foot fishing boat was built for a five-man crew, not just three teenagers.

"Me?" yelled Andrew over the roar of the wind. "*You* thought it was a good idea too."

"Shut up and row," said Philip. At 17, sometimes he wished he were more of a leader, like Andrew. It was almost pitch dark, and it was pelting rain by the bucketful.

"We're not getting any closer," said John. With one hand on the tiller and the other clutching a clay bowl, he desperately swept water overboard. "Oh, *No!*" John watched helplessly as a huge wave bore down on them from the side. If he had the boat properly headed into the wind instead of toward shore, they would ride up over it. Instead, this one looked sure to swamp the boat.

"Philip, quick!" yelled Andrew, "Grab the bow rope!"

"Why?" yelled Philip. But he let loose of the oar and leaned over to grab for the rope anyway—whereupon the wave promptly washed him sputtering out of the boat.

John had a death grip on the tiller, which he realized was a bad idea as it began to sink out of sight. He started thrashing in the water desperately.

"John!" yelled Andrew.

John thrashed.

"*John!*" yelled Andrew again.

"What?" he gasped, thrashing.

"Stand up."

John touched bottom and stood in almost shoulder-high water.

Philip was already standing in the churning water, which was chest-high on his taller frame.

"Did you get the bow rope?" said Andrew.

"Yes," said Philip, waving the free end of it. "But how are we going to get this thing to shore without waking up the whole town to help?"

"My dad is going to be *so* mad at me," moaned John, as another wave washed over his head.

"Yeah, I can hear him now," said Andrew, as he reached John to steady him in the water. "They'll be able to hear old man Zebedee yelling at you from the other side of the lake. They don't call him Big Thunder for nothing."[1]

1

AT THE BACK GATE

FRIDAY, 28 FEBRUARY AD 27, 10:00 AM

"Well hello! Who's this? If it isn't my little John, all the way from Galilee! My, how tall you are! You've sprouted up like a weed! Where's your father? And who is this young man? I suppose you've brought me some smoked and salted fish again? It's been too long since I've seen you! What, a donkey? You must have four bushels of fish loaded onto the poor thing. You're not going to be able to sell all *that* at the Fish Gate before Sabbath starts this evening! And you're going to need a place to sleep tonight, that's for sure! Now you tie that poor thing up to the post over there; I'll not have any beast leaving his droppings in *my* courtyard! Bring in your sacks, and let's see what you've brought."

John blushed. Gabby Gabriela was the lead household servant of Caiaphas in Jerusalem, and she'd been in charge of the house ever since Caiaphas was appointed high priest. She always talked like this, spouting rapid fire questions before anyone had a chance to slip in an answer.

"I—uh—my dad sent me up all by myself this time, ma'am," said John "And I brought my friend Andrew with me.

I'm afraid he and I got ourselves into a heap of trouble with our folks, and we have to work off the debts we've run up. And I have to make a guilt offering in the temple, and I've never done that before."

"We're looking to sell the donkey, too, ma'am," said Andrew, feeling awkward. "My brother Simon says we're feeding too many donkeys."

Gabriela laughed. "Well, let's see what we can do. But I'm afraid I'll not be needing any donkeys today!"

Andrew tied up the donkey, and the two young men carried the burlap sacks into the tiled lower courtyard, which was separated from a large higher courtyard set off by a railing. John opened up one of the sacks and spread out the fish on a stone table.

Gabriela inspected them closely. "Oh my, these look nice! Where'd you get these? They didn't come from that new processing plant at Bethsaida, did they? I don't trust those people. They say they know the right way to do fish, but you just never know, these days!"

"Oh, no ma'am," said John. "My own family caught these fish, and we had them dried, smoked, and salted at the big plant in Magdala. We picked them up when they were ready five days ago, and brought them straight here."

"That's right, ma'am," said Andrew.

"Well I'm glad you did. You can trust those folk in Magdala. And the Lord is smiling on you today! It so happens the chief has called a great feast for all his political friends for next week and I'll be needing a big bunch of food. I just might be able to take the whole lot of these off your hands. Let me call Caleb out here, and he'll weigh them out for us. If there's not too many of them, I'll pay the standard price for the whole lot. Naomi! Take some water outside for these lads' donkey, that's a dear."

"Oh, thank you, ma'am!" exclaimed John. He wasn't really certain what Gabriela considered the "standard price," but he remembered that of all the places he and his father and big brother James had gone to sell fish, the back courtyard of the high priest was where their father had done the least haggling.

———•●●●●———

"Hey, that was easy. She's a nice lady," said Andrew, as they entered the street and Naomi shut the gate behind them.

"Yeah, you're right," said John. "But she talks too fast for me. And her boss is crabby."

"You've seen the high priest?"

"A couple times. He prob'ly knows me by sight,[2] but he's never spoken to my dad or me. The servants are all afraid of him 'cause he's head of the Supreme Council. But not Gabriela. She just calls him chief."

"Well, I'm glad she's the one buying the food," Andrew said. "That fellow Caleb didn't seem very friendly, like he had a bad day, or doesn't like Galileans or something."

"Yeah, his uncle Malchus is chief of staff for the high priest, and he prob'ly wants a more important job," said John. "Come on, let's go over to the Essene Gate and see if we can sell your donkey today. I've seen people selling horses and camels outside there sometimes."

"Which way is it? You know your way around Jerusalem better than I do," said Andrew.

"Oh, it's not far from here. I hope you can get a good price. Did I get a good price for the fish?" John jingled the sack of Jewish shekel coins he was holding.

"Don't *do* that!" Andrew said. "You want someone to stick a knife in you and take your money? Put that inside your clothes where no one can see it!"

"Ouch, you're right," said John as he hid the coin sack.

"You got a real good price. She paid the same you would've got selling 'em one fish at a time at the Fish Gate. She could just as well have paid you the bulk weight price instead."

The two young men wended their way from the high priest's palace, through the winding streets of the Essene Sector and out the southern gate at the junction of the Lower City and the Essene section of the Upper City. There they saw an open sewer line carved into the rock, running alongside a narrow road leading down the slope into the Hinnom valley. Near the bottom were horses and donkeys tied up, several camels, and a few servants looking after livestock.

Andrew approached one of the men there. "Do you know if there's anyone looking to buy a real good pack donkey?" he asked, speaking in his own language, Aramaic.

The man replied, but speaking in Greek. "You can tie your donkey up over there, if you like. Do you need someone to watch over him?"

Andrew quickly switched to Greek. "Oh, no, thank you. But do you know if anyone is looking to buy a good hard-working pack donkey?"

"No. I have just arrived here from Alexandria in Egypt, and my brothers have gone to see if we can find lodging in the Upper City," the man said. "But I have found that we will probably have to stable our horses in the Lower City, because the Essenes will not allow livestock to pass through their portion of the Upper City."

"Is that true?" said Andrew. "We just walked through there with my donkey, and we did not have any trouble."

"I am told that a Bedouin traveler attempted to pass through there last week with his camel, and barely escaped with his life," the man said. "They were trying to stone him, but some Roman soldiers came and rescued him."

John joined the conversation, speaking in Greek. "We did see two Roman soldiers on duty inside the gate when we passed through. Maybe that is why it is so peaceful there right now."

As they were talking, a small boy perhaps nine years old approached. He was barefoot and wearing a threadbare tunic that was at least a size too small for him. Speaking in Aramaic he said, "Misters, can I watch over your donkey while you do your business? I can watch him till sunset for just one lepton!"[3]

"I don't think we need you for that, lad," said Andrew. "But if you can find someone who wants to buy a donkey, I can give you a couple of lepta. In fact, if we make a sale, I can give you a commission on the sale price."

"Oh, great!" exclaimed the boy. "I can do that, misters, I can do that! Wait right here and I'll run into the city and bring someone back right away! Okay?"

Andrew laughed. "And what is your name, young man?"

"I am Hezekiah son of Malchiel who is no longer with us. I live in the Lower City with my mother, two little brothers, and three sisters."

"Has your father died?" asked John.

"We don't know," said Hezekiah. "He went on a short trading journey more than a year ago and hasn't returned."

"I'm sorry about that, Hezekiah," said Andrew. "All right, we will wait for you here one hour. I am Andrew son of Jonah, and this is John son of Zebedee. We live in Galilee."

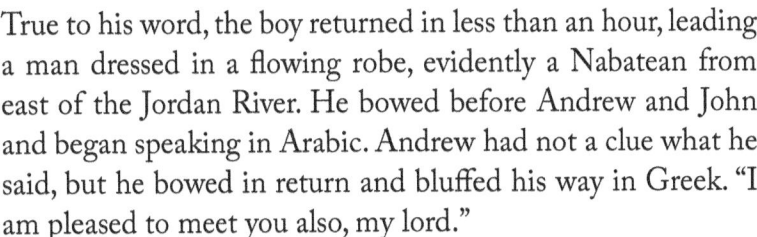

True to his word, the boy returned in less than an hour, leading a man dressed in a flowing robe, evidently a Nabatean from east of the Jordan River. He bowed before Andrew and John and began speaking in Arabic. Andrew had not a clue what he said, but he bowed in return and bluffed his way in Greek. "I am pleased to meet you also, my lord."

That had no effect on the man. Andrew tried the same sentence in Aramaic, but that had no more effect than the Greek. It was evident from the furrows in each man's brow that neither understood the other.

Then Hezekiah piped up. "Mister Andrew, sir, I know Arabic and I can translate for you! He says he is Malichus from Petra and he is honored to meet you and to see if he can help you with your donkey."

Then he translated Andrew's Aramaic greeting into Arabic for the Nabatean, adding "Andrew, son of Jonah." Both Andrew and John noticed Andrew's name added into the greeting, and their esteem of the shrewd young boy went up a couple of notches. The lad had evidently done this before.

And so the bartering began. Malichus checked the donkey's teeth and asked if he had a habit of kicking people. With Hezekiah translating, he said, "My lord, I am sorry you have been burdened by a donkey so young that has never been ridden. But to assist you in your need today I will be happy to take him off your hands and give him a new home, and I won't charge you a single lepton."

Uh oh. Andrew knew now that he was in for a tough bartering session. He countered with an offer to sell the donkey to Malichus for twice what it was worth. But Malichus was an astute bargainer, and within 20 minutes he had reduced the price to the absolute minimum Andrew would accept.

Then Andrew thought of another ploy. He asked for payment of a translator's fee, which he valued at four times what such a fee would normally be. To his surprise, Malichus agreed to pay the full amount. Hezekiah's eyes were glistening as he translated this exchange.

Andrew, John, and Hezekiah watched as Malichus led the donkey up towards the Essene Gate.

When he was out of earshot Hezekiah said, "I think he would've paid more money than that. He's been in town for a month buying stuff, and he needs at least three more donkeys to carry it all before he can go home to Petra."

"I think you're right about the price, Hezzy," said Andrew. "I got more than I would've in Galilee, but I didn't know how to get any more out of Malichus. But how do you know so much about his business?"

"Yeah," said John, "and how'd you get so good at Arabic?"

"Oh he's been staying near my house," Hezekiah said. "I've been hanging out with his son who's about my age, and showing him 'round the Lower City. There's lots of Arabs living there among us. Some of their kids are my best friends. We talk Arabic a lot, but not 'round my mom." Hezekiah fingered the two Roman denarius coins he had just earned for his translation services, which would be two day's wages for a Roman soldier.

Andrew asked him, "What do you know about taking livestock through the Essene sector? The man who was here earlier said you can get stoned for that!"

"Oh, that would be the Essene Zadokites, the wannabe priests in their white robes," Hezekiah said. "They get *really* mad about camels. The Essenes built that latrine up there by the wall and that ritual bath near it, so they could be ritually clean before they go into Jerusalem. Same reason they built this sewer line: they don't wanna step in any dirty water or animal droppings after they come from the bath."

"Thanks," said Andrew. "How do you learn all this stuff?"

"Well," said Hezekiah, "even though I'm just a kid, they let me in at the Synagogue of David, 'cause I'm head of the family now. Or at least I will be, when I'm old enough to become a son of the law.[4] I hear a lot of interesting stuff from the men when they're talking after the synagogue meeting."

"That's great," said Andrew. "Okay, Mister Hezekiah son of Malchiel, it's time for me to pay your commission on the sale. Good work!" Andrew gave him his share of the sale price, and put the rest of the denarii he had gained into a small sack which he put away.

"Oh, thanks, thanks, guys," Hezekiah exclaimed. "I'm gonna run home now, but I'll be watching for you guys if you come to Jerusalem again!"

And off he ran like a shot from a sling. John later found out that when Hezekiah caught up with Malichus, he squeezed another denarius out of him as a finder's fee. The boy was holding maybe enough money to buy himself a new tunic that would actually fit him, but John and Andrew suspected it would be used instead to feed his family.

"Well," John said, "it's my turn to say it: 'Wow, that was easy.' Look, it's only a couple hours past noon! We can make it back to the temple court to buy turtledoves and make our guilt offerings at the evening sacrifice!"

"We can buy the doves, but we can't offer our sacrifices today," said Andrew.

"Why not?"

"I just shook hands with a foreigner, and a Nabatean at that," said Andrew. "I'm gonna be ritually unclean until sundown, and won't be able to enter the temple for a sacrifice."

"Oh yeah," said John. Then after a pause he asked, "Is that written in the law of Moses?"

"Um—Well I'm not really sure, but that's what the Pharisees teach."

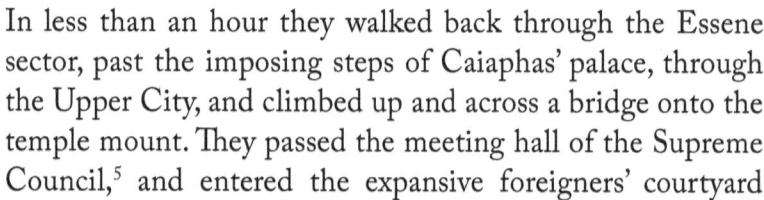

In less than an hour they walked back through the Essene sector, past the imposing steps of Caiaphas' palace, through the Upper City, and climbed up and across a bridge onto the temple mount. They passed the meeting hall of the Supreme Council,⁵ and entered the expansive foreigners' courtyard where a few sheep and goats were tied and even a couple of oxen.

There were tables set up by moneychangers and by merchants selling turtledoves and pigeons. Between the merchants and the temple there was a railing—a stone balustrade with a carved marble sign set into it. Beyond the railing was the temple itself, with separate entrances for women and men. Two temple police were guarding each entrance.

John said, "Andrew, you read Greek better than I do—what does that sign actually say?"

"Well, Philip's the expert, but I can read it," said Andrew. He moved closer to the sign and read out the words:[6]

> NO STRANGER IS TO ENTER WITHIN THE BALUSTRADE ROUND THE TEMPLE AND ENCLOSURE. WHOEVER IS CAUGHT WILL BE RESPONSIBLE TO HIMSELF FOR HIS DEATH, WHICH WILL ENSUE.

"That's what I thought," said John. "If an Arab or a Persian went in there, the chief priests in the Supreme Council wouldn't have to wait for permission from the Romans to finish him off. Look, there's a pile of rocks to throw at them."

Andrew said, "Oh yeah. Okay, Let's buy some pigeons."

"Are you going to exchange all your denarii for shekels?" John asked.

"No, only enough to pay the temple taxes," he said. "My brother Simon can get a better exchange rate in Bethsaida."

The two young men went to a moneychanger's table and Andrew bought a few Jewish half-shekels, because Roman money wasn't accepted in the temple. Then they bought four turtledoves for sacrifice, even though they were a bit more expensive than the pigeons they could have used if they wished. Then for a little extra, they obtained a small cage to hold the doves until the next day.

"Okay, we're done here for today," said Andrew.

"Yea, let's go over to Caiaphas' place," said John. "We'll be safe there in the courtyard, and Gabriela said we could sleep there tonight… and I'll bet she feeds us supper, too."

2

AT THE ALTAR

SATURDAY, 1 MARCH AD 27, 7:00 AM

Early next morning, the two young men stood in the temple watching the priests stand at the elaborate raised altar and conduct the Sabbath morning sacrifice ritual. Behind the priests was the great curtain separating the Holy of Holies, which no one would enter until the Day of Atonement. The young men had already dropped their payment of the temple tax into the locked offering box in a side passageway, and were standing in line waiting for the time when the priests would accept their guilt offerings.

The time came quickly. Andrew gave two doves to an assisting priest, saying, "This is for a guilt offering.[7] I have sinned against God and family and community by leading them into error and causing loss, and I am making reparation in accord with the Law for the damage I have done." While he handed the doves over, he discretely slipped the priest a half-shekel. Without that customary bribe, they might encounter an overly-critical inspection of the sacrificial animal for blemishes, and have their offering rejected.

John followed Andrew's lead. He said, "This is for a guilt offering. I have sinned against God and family and community by taking my father's boat and causing loss. I am making reparation in accord with the Law for the damage I have done." He handed over the expected bribe.

For each of them the priest intoned, "Your offering is accepted as ransom for your life and atonement with God for your sin."

They watched solemnly as the priest at the altar killed the doves and splattered the blood, and then turned to leave. Stepping outside the temple, John said, "I thought I'd feel better after making the atonement sacrifice, but I feel worse. I still feel ashamed, and I don't know if I'm right with God or not."

Andrew thought long and hard. "I think I know what you mean. I thought I'd feel liberated, but I still feel weighed down. Maybe we'll feel better later."

"Let's go down to the Lower City and go to synagogue," John said. "If we hurry we can find the Synagogue of David and see Hezekiah again. We can't leave for home before tonight anyway because of the Sabbath."

"Good idea," said Andrew. "Let's see if we can find the Huldah Gates. I've never been there."

The Huldah Gates were down a stairwell and underneath the court of the foreigners, and led out to the Lower City. Coming out of the gates back into the bright sun, they walked south a bit and got directions from a man who told them how to get to the Synagogue of David. It was well inside the grounds of what had once been the ancient City of David, situated on Mount Zion. People were already filing in, so they followed and stood in the midst of the other men.

Andrew whispered to John excitedly, "Look! There's Nathanael over there! What's he doing in Jerusalem? Maybe Philip is here too!" John stood up on his toes so he could see tall Nathanael's head sticking up above the other men, but he couldn't tell if Nathanael saw him or not.

The service began, and they followed along with the familiar ritual: morning blessing and verses of song followed by the Shema,[8] when everyone said,

> Hear, O Israel! The Lord is our God, the Lord is one! You shall love the Lord your God with all your heart and with all your soul and with all your might!

Next came blessings and praise, and then the Torah—the Law of Moses—was carried around the congregation. The Rabbi read in Hebrew from the passage assigned for the day:

> Moses said, "The Lord your God will raise up for you a prophet like me from among you—from your brethren. You shall listen to him. This is according to all that you asked of the Lord your God in Horeb on the day of the assembly, saying 'Let me not hear again the voice of the Lord my God; let me not see this great fire anymore, or I will die.' The Lord said to me, 'They have spoken well. I will raise up a prophet like you from among their brethren, and I will put my words in his mouth, and he will speak to them all that I command him.'"[9]

Then the Rabbi introduced the speaker who would read and comment on the Haftarah—the reading from the Prophets. He was an Essene, although not a priest. Everyone was wondering what the man might say. The Rabbi gave him the scroll of Isaiah, and he read from the Hebrew script:

> The distressed will soon be set free, and will not die in the dungeon, nor will his bread be lacking. I am the

Lord your God, who stirs up the sea and its waves roar—the Lord of Heaven's Armies is my name. I have put my words in your mouth and have covered you with the shadow of my hand, to establish the heavens, to found the earth, and to say to Zion, "you are my people."[10]

The man handed back the scroll and sat down in a chair near the Rabbi. All eyes in the congregation were upon him, and he began to speak in Aramaic:

"This scripture will be fulfilled very soon, perhaps even today. The prophet like Moses will come to herald the Anointed One of God. The days of the captivity of Israel will come to an end. In the last days the nations will wage war against Mount Zion. They will think they have won, but that will be in their imagination. At that time the Lord will lead a great army into battle in command of all nature's forces. Every opponent in heaven and on earth will be subdued. Then the Lord will rule the world from Mount Zion. All kings and nations will confess that the Lord of Heaven's Armies is the King of Glory. His kingdom will reign forever."

Hardly a sound was heard in the Synagogue for a long, pregnant pause. Then the Rabbi broke the silence and led the congregation in the closing Psalm 145, which ends with the words, "My mouth will speak the praise of the Lord, and let every creature bless his holy name. Blessed be the Lord and blessed be his name forever and ever."[11]

The Rabbi dismissed the people, and a group of men gathered around the speaker, gesticulating and talking excitedly in Hebrew. Andrew and John were avoiding them as they began to file out, when Hezekiah came up and tugged at John's elbow. "Oh, there you are, Hezzy!" said John. "I was looking for you but I didn't see you."

"What do you think of what the speaker said?" asked Hezekiah. "Do you think he means the new prophet that's down by the Jordan River? Did you see the prophet when you came up from Galilee?"

"I haven't heard of any new prophet," said John, "but we came on the high road through Samaria, not the low road along the Jordan."

"Oh, everyone in the Lower City is talking about him!" Hezekiah said. "He's saying that the word of God has fallen on him and he's calling for repentance, and dunking people in the river. He calls it a 'baptism of repentance' to prepare the way for the kingdom of God."

Nathanael caught up with them outside. "Hi, guys! Philip told me you guys went to Jerusalem, but I didn't expect I'd bump into you here!"

"We were just talking about what that speaker said in synagogue," said Andrew. "What do you think about it?"

"I wouldn't go by what that guy said. Those are the same things the Essenes have been saying every day for the past hundred years," said Nathanael.

John asked Nathanael, "So what do you think about the new prophet down by the Jordan? Did you see him? Hezekiah just told us about him!"

"I didn't see this so-called 'prophet,'" said Nathanael, "but I heard about him while I was traveling up to here on the road from Cana."

A short man from the congregation had been drawn to their conversation, and he was followed by a young boy about as tall as Hezekiah. He interrupted, "Gentlemen, you sound like you might be Galileans. I'm James son of Alpheus and this is my son Judas Thaddeus. We're from Ephraim, but I have relatives in Galilee. Have you heard that new prophet down by the Jordan?"

"It's an honor to meet you, James," said Andrew. "I'm Andrew son of Jonah, and this is John son of Zebedee, and this is Nathanael son of Tholmai,[12] and you're right, we're from Galilee. And this is Hezekiah son of Malchiel, who lives right here. And no, we haven't heard the prophet. What do you think of him?"

"I don't know what to think," said James, "I've a mind to travel out there and hear him for myself. I've been hearing conflicting reports. One person says he's the Anointed One—the Messiah—and another says he denies being the Messiah. Then other people say he's the prophet like Moses."

"John and I are getting ready to go that way tomorrow," said Andrew. "Maybe we'll take the low road and get a chance to see him."

"Oh, I wish I could go with you!" exclaimed Hezekiah. "But I gotta stay here and take care of my brothers and sisters."

"Tell you what," said James, "why don't you let me buy you all a meal over at the little inn where I'm staying? The food is really good there. We can talk some more about this prophet and what all this might mean."

That sounded like a great idea to the rest, and they set off to the Upper City. James led the way with Andrew and Nathanael, while John, Thaddeus, and Hezekiah followed behind.

As they walked, James said, "I just came up from Ephraim with a new curtain to replace the one hanging behind the collection box in the temple—it was beginning to look faded. That's a little part I play to fulfill my duties as a Levite. But the Sadducees in the temple don't always like outsiders coming in to help. They'd rather have money."

"That's interesting," said Nathanael. "My family makes wool rugs. My cousin Matthias and I came up to Jerusalem a week ago with some of our rugs, and we sold all of them, so we're ready to go back to Cana. I'm 18 now, so I make most of the trips here for my father. But it is a little dangerous, even though my cousin travels with me."

"It's a long story why John and I are here," Andrew said. "The short version is that John and I and Nathanael's friend Philip stole John's father's boat for a joy ride in the middle of the night. We thought we might come back with some fish and be heroes. Instead we ran into a big storm that sank the boat, and we had to wake up the whole village to help us salvage it and haul it on shore. But we lost old Zebedee's long-line net we use when our families work together to bring in the big fish hauls. So we're here to earn some money to pay for the damages, and this morning we made our guilt offerings in the temple."

"That's quite a story," laughed James. "I'd like to hear the long version some day."

Nathanael updated Andrew on the comings and goings of his friend Philip, who had been to Jerusalem earlier and had already paid his debt from their escapade on the lake.

While the older men were talking, the younger three lads were having their own conversation as they brought up the rear. Hezekiah said, "I like looking at the big houses and buildings in the Upper City, but the people there chase me away. D'you like staying there, Judas?"

"Oh, just call me Tad; that's what everyone calls me," said Judas Thaddeus James. "I love coming up to Jerusalem. My dad's been bringing me along to show me what he does here. He meets with the other Levites to plan for the upkeep of the temple. I'm almost 13 years old, and in a few months my dad's gonna make me a son of the law."

"I had that 'honor' a year ago," said John, "and today I had to make my own sacrifice at the temple, 'cause I stole my dad's boat to go joy-riding. Boy, did I get in trouble."

"Oh yeah?" chimed Tad and Hezekiah together. "Tell us all about it," said Tad. But before John reached the end of his story, they arrived at the inn. The food was indeed wonderful, and John had a chance to tell his whole story, including the embarrassing part where he thought he was going to drown, but all he had to do was stand up.

James arranged for John and Andrew and Nathanael to stay for the night at the inn, while Hezekiah had to run home, "before my mother worries herself sick," as he said.

The remaining group continued to talk until evening. As they parted to go to their sleeping pallets, Nathanael said to James, "Andrew and I and John have decided we're definitely going down the river road to listen to this 'baptizer' and see what's happening there. Who knows? Maybe it really is time for God to come and set things straight."

"I need to return to Ephraim," James said, "but I will probably try to come down to hear him a few days after you get there. May God speed you on your journey, if I don't see you in the morning before you leave."

3

A Voice Cries Out

Wednesday, 5 March AD 27, 8:00 am

Rain. Not hard rain, but steady rain. And not warm rain, but rather chilly. It had been raining for two days. At a fork in the road, Nathanael's cousin Matthias had taken their two donkeys with him to travel with a group taking a westerly path as far as the village of Nain. Then Nathanael, Andrew, and John had taken the easterly path to Bethabara[13] along with some twenty others who had come to hear the new prophet. They had made a difficult crossing of the Jordan River south of the Sea of Galilee, and were wet and cold and miserable.

And now fog. The rain had stopped an hour ago, and the sun was struggling to dispel the swirling fog. They were standing on a sandy bank next to a quiet eddy of the river with about 50 others, shivering and waiting for the Baptist. His assistants said he would prophesy from a hillock just above the sandy bank.

A drift of thick cold fog swept in to obscure both the riverbank and the hillock, then suddenly opened up. Standing there above them was an unkempt, wild-looking man, barefoot and dressed in a garment of camel's hair fastened with a leather belt.[14] The crowd was hushed, and the fierce man was silent as he looked at them.

"A VOICE CRIES OUT!" he thundered.

Andrew and Nathanael were startled. John almost jumped.

"Clear the way in the wilderness for the Lord!

"Smooth out a highway in the desert for our God!

"Every valley shall be lifted up! Every mountain and hill shall be laid low! The rough ground shall be leveled, and the rugged places made smooth. Then the glory of the Lord will be revealed, and all mankind together will see it. The mouth of the Lord has spoken!"[15]

John felt his sphincter muscles tighten, and the hair on the back of his neck stand up.

The Baptist continued in a more moderate tone: "Today this writing of the prophet Isaiah is being fulfilled in your very ears. Now when Isaiah says 'Every valley shall be lifted,' the interpretation of the word is that all of you who are lowly and confess your sins will be lifted up. And the interpretation of 'Every mountain and hill shall be laid low' is that all you who think yourselves righteous and lordly and refuse to repent will be brought down.

"REPENT, for the kingdom of God is at hand! As for me, I baptize you in water as a sign of repentance. But after me there is One who is coming, even already in the land, who will baptize you with Holy Spirit, and with fire. He is mightier than I, and I am not fit to stoop down and untie his sandal. His winnowing fork is in his hand, to thoroughly clear his threshing floor and to gather the wheat into his barn; but he will burn up the chaff with unquenchable fire.[16]

"Therefore repent today and be baptized, and go forth from here to bear fruit in keeping with repentance!"

When he finished speaking, the Baptist and one of his younger assistants moved toward the river, and walked out in the water to waist depth. A low murmur arose from the crowd as some drifted into a line to be baptized, while others hesitated.

Nathanael spoke quietly to Andrew and John: "Well, maybe he's a quack, or a lunatic, or a real prophet; I can't tell. But I see no harm in repenting. I could use some repentance."

The other two nodded, and joined the line behind Nathanael. The Baptist was talking quietly with each person as they presented themselves, then he and his assistant would immerse each one into the river then lift them back up out of the water.

When it was Nathanael's turn, he waded into the water. As he approached, the Baptist looked him in the eyes, and proclaimed loudly, "Look, a pillar of the New Jerusalem!"

Nathanael was taken aback, and for once he had no snappy response. The Baptist lowered his voice. "And what do you confess today, my son?"

Nathanael had to clear his head of the Baptist's strange assault, and return to what he had already purposed to say: "I confess to being sometimes arrogant toward others, and repent of all my unknown sins."

Nathanael was baptized, and Andrew was next in line. The Baptist spoke in a more normal tone: "What, another pillar of Jerusalem? What do you confess, my son?"

"I confess to leading my brothers astray into sin," said Andrew, and he was baptized in the same manner as Nathanael.

Now it was John's turn. The Baptist looked him in the eyes, and exclaimed, "JOSEPH!"

"No, my name is John son of Zebedee," said John in wonder.

"Yes, and my name is John son of Zacharias," answered the Baptist, "but I have received a vision which concerns you. In this vision I saw the sun giving the moon to you, after which eleven pillars will fall, one at a time, until your pillar is the only one standing. And after that you will work in the spirit of the patriarch Joseph, to bring forgiveness and love for one another among your brethren. May you bear your mission well. Now what have you to say for yourself?"

Like Nathanael, John had to clear his mind before he could speak: "I have shamed my father and my family by causing him loss and disgrace, and I repent."

As John was being dunked in the water he had a momentary flash of terror as he recalled the squall on the Sea of Galilee when the waves were washing over his head. But then strong hands lifted him out of the water and he was steadied, just as Andrew had steadied him in the waves, and he walked back to the shore overwhelmed.

John and Andrew and Nathanael were sitting contemplatively at the foot of the hillock beside the river. The Baptist had retreated into the bush-land beyond the hillock, and the crowd that had been baptized was drifting away. The Baptist's young assistant came over and joined them.

"Hello," he said. "I'm Daniel. I've been a disciple of John the Baptist for three months now. Not many people were here today; sometimes we've had as many as 400 at once."

"That's a lot," said Nathanael. "I'm Nathanael, and this is Andrew and John. Do you know what all that talk of 'pillars' was about?"

"No, I was hoping you knew something about it," said Daniel. "The prophet often has individual messages for the ones he's baptizing, and once in a while he sees a vision. But he's not always given the meaning of the vision. More often, he just looks at a person, and tells the person about a sin he has committed that needs repentance."

John asked, "How did you get to be a disciple?"

"I just didn't leave here after he baptized me," said Daniel. "The prophet doesn't ask for disciples; he thinks a Greater One is coming very soon, and that his own mission here is just temporary. He sends people away to 'bear fruit in keeping with repentance,' as he says. There aren't very many of us here, only seven right now."

Nathanael asked, "He said something today about 'One coming,' and that the man was 'already in the land.' What's that all about?"

"He's been saying that, or something like it, for the last month," said Daniel. "He doesn't talk about it except when he's preaching. It started a month ago when something very strange happened while he was baptizing someone."

"Oh, what was that?" said Andrew.

"A man came to be baptized, and the prophet said, 'No, I need to be baptized by you!' But the man insisted, and then when he came up out of the water I heard some thunder, or maybe it was a voice, and the prophet was looking up into the sky. He was very agitated. We haven't seen the man since then."[17]

"This is strange and disturbing stuff," said Nathanael. "I want to go up to Bethsaida and bring my friend Philip back to hear some more from this prophet. Something is going on here."

"I'm thinking I'd like to stay here for a while and learn more," said Andrew. "Nate, can I ask you to bring my brother Simon back here? This is something he should hear."

"If Andrew is staying, I'll stay here with him," said John. "But it would be great if my big brother James could come and hear it too. Nate, maybe you could talk him into it."

"Okay, Okay! I'll just tell Simon to leave his new wife behind, and I'll tell James to stop fishing, and I'll bring the whole town with me!" said Nathanael.

Then he settled down. "Sorry, that was unfair. Of course I'll bring them if they'll come. And maybe some of the other fisherfolk will end up coming too. Look for me in about a week."

"Thanks, Nate," said Andrew, and he turned to talk to the Baptist's disciple. "Daniel, what should we do if we stay here? Just keep a low profile?"

"Oh, no guys," said Daniel. "I can show you where the prophet is staying. It's not far. But I hope you don't mind eating locusts. The people coming for baptism bring us food, but sometimes we run out."

"We've got at least a week's supply of food," said Andrew. "We'll be glad to share."

The two younger men said their goodbyes to Nathanael, and entrusted him with the profits from their Jerusalem journey to take to father Zebedee and father Jonah. Then they followed Daniel up the slope and along a trail into the riverside bushes, talking as they went.

Andrew said, "Daniel, I thought the Bethabara Ferry was around here somewhere. We sure had a time crossing the river!"

Daniel said, "Yes, the ferry is just up-river, but it's shut down now until caravan season starts again. And if you use the ferry a lot, you'll need a pocketful of shekels. They make a ton of money when the caravans come through. The place we're staying is actually where the ferry workers live, and we're watching over it till they come back. There's just one guard they left behind to make sure nobody messes with the boats. He stays in a cabin down by the river."

They arrived at a clearing that held two smallish houses, one of them barred shut and vacant. John the Baptist emerged from the other one and waved to the young men to welcome them in. As it turned out, the Baptist wasn't really fierce—he just *looked* fierce.

Young John Zebedee finally got up the nerve to ask him a question. "Prophet, Tell me again about the vision you had of the pillars."

"Not much left to tell. Strange vision. I saw the sun give the moon to a pillar, which represented a man, and the man was supposed to take care of the moon, and the moon was supposed to take care of the man. Very confusing. There were twelve pillars with names on them I could not read, but when I saw your face, I knew that the twelfth pillar was yours. The pillars were for the New Jerusalem—or maybe a new temple—that is going to be built, perhaps soon. Does any of this mean anything to you?"

"No sir," John said, "but it does sound a little like one of the dreams that patriarch Joseph had when he was young. He almost got himself killed by his eleven brothers over that dream." [18]

"Ah, very good," responded the Baptist, "I see we have ourselves a young scholar of the books of Moses here. I have something you might want to read that may have something about pillars in it. Do you read Hebrew?"

"Oh yes, sir. My father was very strict about our Hebrew lessons at the synagogue, and just as strict about learning proper Greek from our grammar books. He said we'd never know the Lord if we didn't know Hebrew, and we'd never know business if we didn't know Greek."

The Baptist rummaged around in a leather case that was lying next to the wall, and pulled out a tattered scroll. "Ah, here it is! This is part of an inspired commentary on the book of Isaiah—a *pesher*—that I was copying in the scriptorium at Qumran. In fact, this is the very scroll I was working on when the hand of the Lord fell on me to proclaim his word. When I came upon the words, '*a voice crying out, in the wilderness,*' I could write no further without my hand shaking violently. They kicked me out of the scriptorium and out of the Essene party, and this was after I had given them the entire family fortune."

"Wow," said John. "How did you come to be in such a place?"

"My father and mother were already elderly when I was born. But my father was a priest of the temple, and before he and my mother died they taught me all the things a priest does and the way he does it.

"But I got a good glimpse from the inside of how corrupt the priesthood of the temple really was, among the Sadducees and even the Pharisees. So I ran away into the desert and applied to join the Essene community at Qumran, where they were teaching purity for priests. The Essenes refuse to have anything to do with the priests at the temple, who are not only corrupt, but also come from the wrong family lineage."

"I've heard about that Qumran place," said John. "Doesn't it take three years to join?"

"Ah, you surprise me! You know so much! Yes, three years, and many times of dipping yourself in the ritual baths. But they got one thing right: It doesn't matter how many times you wash yourself with water—if you have not cleansed your heart, the water will do nothing for you."

"So were you accepted?"

"No, they rejected me and turned me away on the eve of my final purification rite."

Andrew had been listening attentively. He asked, "And they wouldn't give you back your family fortune?"

"No, they had already hidden the money away in their secret places to be used when it is time to arm themselves for the final war against the Romans and the wicked. As if the Lord of Heaven's Armies actually needed their help.

"Here John, take this scroll," the Baptist continued, "and return it before you leave. It has some good points and some bad points. Remember it was written by men who believe that if they do all the right things they will be without sin. They have forgotten the words of King David who wrote in his psalm, 'There is no one who is righteous, no not one.'" [19]

4

Pharisees and Sadducees

Thursday, 6 March AD 27, 8:00 am

It was morning again at the riverside, but today was bright and sunny. Daniel and two other disciples of the Baptist, along with John and Andrew, were waiting for the prophet's arrival. On the night before, after the Baptist had heard the story of the sinking of Zebedee's boat, he decided Andrew would take the first turn at assisting with the baptisms. John, on the other hand, would have the whole day available with just one instruction: read the scroll he had been loaned the night before.

    Some one hundred people were gathered, and a few stragglers were still crossing the river. Then five finely dressed men astride horses appeared, riding downriver from the ferry crossing. They were attended by at least ten servants, and were arrayed in the fine silks and raiment of the ruling class of Jerusalem. From their adornments, there were evidently three of the Pharisee party and two of the Sadducee party, though none of them were priests.

The five dismounted behind the crowd, and left the servants in charge of the horses. The crowd of pilgrims parted for them so they could come up to the very front of the gathering. At that very moment, the Baptist appeared atop the stony hillock.

The prophet stood there for a moment as the crowd became silent, waiting for him to speak. Then he looked directly at the five finely arrayed men and began to preach:

"YOU BROOD OF VIPERS, who warned you to flee from the wrath to come? *REPENT*, for the kingdom of God is at hand!

"For some of you—indeed, all five of you—have dined at the same table with that miserable kinglet Herod Antipas. He has taken to himself the wife of his brother Philip, which is not lawful for him to do.[20] And did you carefully instruct him in the law, you teachers of the law? Let shame be upon your heads!

"Therefore bear fruit in keeping with repentance, and do not suppose you can say to yourselves, 'We have Abraham for our father,' for I say to you that from these stones God is able to raise up children to Abraham. Indeed the axe is already laid at the root of the trees; and every tree that does not bear good fruit will be cut down and thrown into the fire!"[21]

Turning his attention to the rest of the crowd, he continued his sermon, using much the same words as the previous day. But when he finished speaking, as the crowd followed the Baptist to the water, the five splendidly-dressed men returned to their horses. Their faces were red with rage as they rode off, followed by their retinue of servants.

John was up on the flat roof of the house that the Baptist and his disciples were using. He was soaking up the welcome afternoon warmth of the early March sunshine, and puzzling through some of the faded text on the ragged scroll the Baptist had loaned him. Andrew arrived back from the river, and trudged up the outdoor steps leading to the rooftop.

"Wow, I'm tired," said Andrew. "Daniel says they've baptized as many as 400 people in a single day. I don't know how they do it. We baptized 128 people today, from 10-year-olds to elders, male and female. But the prophet was just as energetic at the end as at the beginning."

"I wonder if he will give me a chance to help him do that?" responded John.

"I dunno, I think you need to be a little taller first. We had trouble lifting up a couple of the heavier men," said Andrew.

Daniel arrived from the bush path, and joined them on the rooftop. Andrew said to him, "That was really bold and startling what the prophet said to those five rich guys!"

"Yeah," said Daniel. "But they got really mad. I hope they don't send back a bunch of soldiers with swords to get even."

"Eww, I didn't think of that," said John. "Do you think that might happen?"

"I hope not. We haven't attracted much attention from soldiers and kings here yet."

Andrew said, "Maybe not. But if word gets around to King Herod of what the Baptist said about him and his new wife, there's going to be trouble. If I were him I'd move from here into Judea or Samaria to get farther away from Herod Antipas' territory."

"You may be right, Andrew," said Daniel. "We'll have to keep our ear to the ground so we know what's up."

John asked, "So how did they get the ferry running, Daniel? They got here without a single spot of mud or water on their clothes."

"I found out about that," Daniel said. "Those guys brought the owner of the ferry down here from Jerusalem with them, along with five of his workers, and paid them very well."

Daniel continued, "Hey John, did you find out anything about the prophet's vision from that scroll you're reading?"

"Not yet," said John "The scroll is badly damaged and it's hard reading. It's going to take me a few more days to get through the whole thing."

"Better you than me," said Andrew. "I have enough trouble even with new scrolls."

5

Samaritans and Soldiers

Friday, 7 March AD 27, 8:00 am

Another sunny day, but fewer people had arrived, for the Sabbath day of rest was near. Daniel was on duty on the eastern approach to greet any who might arrive by way of the caravan trail from Damascus, while John was greeting people as they came up from the river crossing. Just when it looked as if there would be only a couple dozen people for the Baptist's sermon, another group of two dozen or more appeared. John went out to meet them.

"Hello, welcome!" John said. "We are gathering over by this small hill, and the prophet will arrive soon to proclaim the word of God. Did you all come from the same place?"

To John's surprise, there were two Roman soldiers in the group. He was startled, and thought to himself, *"Did those rich guys send soldiers to arrest the Baptist? And how could they have gotten here so quickly?"*

One of the soldiers asked John, "Do you speak Greek?"

"Yes, sir," John said.

The soldier continued in Greek: "As a matter of fact, yes we did, young man. Petronius and I have a fortnight left before we are scheduled to report to duty in Jerusalem, so we decided to come down and hear what this prophet has to say. We left from Sychar in Samaria, and these folk from Sychar felt safer if they travelled with us. There has been talk of bandits on the road."

John said, "Well, we are glad you all came. The Prophet will preach the word of God, and after his sermon he will baptize in water as a sign for those who come in a spirit of repentance."

The Baptist arrived, and surveyed the crowd for a minute or two before he spoke:

"REPENT, for the kingdom of God is at hand! The Most High God, who created heaven and earth has sent me as one who is 'crying aloud in the wilderness,' to proclaim that every valley will be filled and every mountain and hill will be laid low, to make straight a highway for the Lord. Those of you who are poor or humble, and who repent from your sins, will be lifted up. Those of you who are rich or powerful, and who refuse to repent from your sins, will be brought down."

The Baptist continued, tailoring his words to speak to the Samaritans. The Samaritans were normally despised by Jews as members of an impure race, and because they worship God on a mountain instead of in the Temple. Then he ended his sermon rather differently.

"Do any of you have any questions to ask, before you are baptized?" the prophet said.

After a hesitation, one of the Samaritans asked, "Sir, after we are baptized and leave here, what are we to do next?"

"The man who has two tunics to wear is to share with him who has none; and he who has food to eat is to do likewise. Follow these principals in all your affairs and you will do well."

Another man raised his hand and spoke, "Sir, I am a tax collector and despised by many people. What is it that I should do?"

"Collect no more from the people than what you have been ordered to collect."

Then to everyone's surprise, the soldier Petronius spoke up, saying, "And what about us, what should we do?"

"Do not take money from anyone by force. Do not accuse anyone falsely. Be content with the wages you are being paid," said the Baptist.[22]

The evening was chilly, and the three young men—John, Andrew, and Daniel—gathered inside the house with the prophet to review the day's activities.

"When I saw those soldiers," John said, "I thought we were all going to be arrested for sure and thrown into some pit."

"Yeah, we haven't had soldiers here before," said Daniel. "I was surprised that they wanted to be baptized."

"Did you see how each one handed his sword and shield to the other before they went in the water?" Andrew asked. "But they refused to take off their leather armor, so they were still heavy to lift up out of the water."

"Prophet," said John, "today you baptized two soldiers who were not Jews, and not even Samaritans. Are they going to be included in the kingdom of God?"

"I don't know, my son," said the prophet, "but they will never forget today, when they had an encounter with the Most High God, the maker of heaven and earth, and learned that he is a forgiving God. And remember, even though we children of Abraham are the people of God, the Lord is still God of all people in the world, for he created them. Have you not read in the scroll you are reading where the Lord makes an oath upon himself and declares, 'To Me every knee will bow, and every tongue will swear allegiance'?" [23]

"Oh no sir, I haven't read that far yet," said John. "But I did hear it said in synagogue."

Andrew spoke up: "What about the Samaritans? Will they stop their useless worship at Mount Gerizim, or will they still be accursed at the temple by the priests?"

"The Lord has not revealed that to me, my son," said the prophet. "But I have seen a vision of a new temple, made available to all of the true worshippers of God. Its appearance I cannot understand, but it is related in some way to twelve pillars. More than that I cannot say, except that no man whose sin has been forgiven is accursed by God, no matter what the priests say."

He paused, and then continued pensively: "And these words I have just spoken would drive the Essenes crazy, especially my teachers at Qumran. It was well they evicted me."

6

NATHANAEL RETURNS

FRIDAY, 14 MARCH AD 27, 8:00 AM

Today Andrew was on duty as greeter by the riverside, and John was hanging out with him. Nathanael had said he would be back in a week, but he was two days overdue. James son of Alpheus, who they had met in Jerusalem, was at least a week behind the time he said he would come. John had been looking forward to seeing Thaddeus again, and he was eager to see the tall, muscular frame of his big brother James.

Excitedly, John spotted Nathanael about to cross the river. And there was James his brother! He called out, "Ahoy, James!"

"Ahoy, John! You gettin' yourself in trouble again?"

And there was Philip, right behind him, along with the Bashan brothers, two fishermen from Capernaum.

And there was Andrew's brother Simon bringing up the rear, and along with him was his wife Concordia! Andrew called out across the river, "Yo, Simon!"

The river was not as high as it had been when John, Andrew, and Nathanael had first arrived at Bethabara, so Simon did not need to offer help to Concordia as she crossed.

James bounded onto the shore first, and swept his little brother into a big bear hug. "You may not believe this, but Dad really misses you! He was happy when Nate brought us news about you. And of course Mom was her usual worry-wart. She sent you some stuff."

"It's been real interesting here," said John. "I guess I'm a disciple of the Baptist now. He's started to call me 'my son.'"

James laughed. "Look, we've brought a bunch of food for everyone here. We figured you'd be running low by now, so Nate and I and Philip have our packs filled up. We had to hold back a day on leaving while our mom and Philip's mom prepared some special foods."

Andrew greeted Simon and his bride at the river's edge. "Hey, Bro! Hello, Concordia! I wasn't expecting you." Hugs went all around.

Concordia said, "As soon as I found out what all the men were up to, I let Simon know there would be no food for him if he didn't bring his wife along. I've been dying to see this Baptist, and find out what's going on in God's world. And Simon was eager to come see also."

Andrew said, "There haven't been many women who have come out this far into the wilderness in this wintry weather."

"Oh, we won't have any problems staying warm," said Simon. (Concordia glanced at him with a flash in her eye.) "But we can only stay a few days," he continued. "I heard what John said about being a 'disciple,' but I don't think we're going to hang around long enough for the prophet to start calling us sons and daughter."

Nathanael and Philip joined them, and Philip said, "Hey John! Hey Andrew! You guys staying out of trouble?"

Andrew and John both started to talk at once. Then Andrew continued, "Maybe not, Philip. A few days back, the prophet dissed King Herod about his new wife Herodias, and then chewed out some rich Pharisees and Sadducees who came down to hear the prophet. Hey, were they ticked off! Then the very next day two Roman soldiers showed up, and you won't believe what they did!"

"Lemme guess," ventured Nathanael. "They gave all of you a very stern warning and said to never do that again or they'd come back and chop you up into little pieces for breakfast."

"Nope," said Andrew. "They listened to the prophet, and then they got baptized!"

"Oh, now I *know* I gotta hear this guy," said Philip. "When does he start?"

"Oh! Right now!" said John. "Come on, we better hurry before he gets here. He preaches from the rocky knoll over there."

Beon and Bohan, the Bashan brothers from Capernaum, were bemused by all this, and said their hello's while following them up the beach.

The Baptist had been in rare form today, and everyone who had come to hear was baptized, almost a hundred in all. The new arrivals from Galilee, along with John and Andrew, were gathered at the foot of the hill, drying off in the weak sunlight and talking about what the Baptist had said.

Beon asked, of no one in particular, "I heard the prophet say that there was One coming that was greater than himself. Didn't he also say this 'greater one' was 'already in the land'?"

"Yeah, you're right, Beon," said Andrew. "He's been saying that for almost a month and a half. His disciples say that started after a man came to be baptized, and the prophet said that he himself should be baptized by the man. But no one has seen the man since then."

"This 'greater one' that the prophet is talking about could only be the Messiah," said Bohan. "Our family has been waiting for the Messiah to appear, because he will give us back our lands."

"Tell us some more about that," said Nathanael. "What lands are you talking about?"

"Our family is of the tribe of Reuben, and we're a cattle and sheep-raising tribe. We few hold on to the blessing of Moses, when he said, 'Let the tribe of Reuben live, and not die.'[24] Our ancestor Belah owned huge tracts of grazing land in the plains of Bashan, from here to Damascus and beyond. We are descended from Beerah, the Prince of Reuben, who was carried off to Assyria by its king. In fact, my father Bashan is the rightful prince of this land we're standing on.

"The prophet Micah tells of the instruction of God to the Messiah, when he wrote:

> Shepherd your people with your scepter,
> The flock of your inheritance,
> Which dwells by itself in a forest,
> In the midst of fruitful pasture lands.
> Let them feed in Bashan and Gilead,
> As in the days of old."[25]

"So, Bohan, tell me," said Nathanael, "Are you ready to throw away your fishing nets and take up your shepherd's staff and cattle lasso?"

"The truth?"

"Yes, of course."

"I will give up my nets and lines when I see the Messiah take his seat on King David's throne in Jerusalem, not before."

"That's good," said Simon, "for I would surely miss your help in my family's fishing boat."

Beon added, "And unless we see the Messiah, we're only going to be here one more day."

Philip asked, "So, John, what's it like living in the prophet's house?"

"Well," said John, "he's actually a pretty nice guy. And it's not his house; it's just borrowed from the ferry crew. I suppose they're coming back soon to reopen the ferry in the spring, so he might have to find somewhere else to live."

"Do you think he would mind one more person?"

"Oh, there's plenty of room for more. But he might give you an assignment to help out with the baptisms. My assignment is to read a scroll he loaned me and report back to him about it."

"Okay, I'll follow you when you go there, and you can tell me more about this scroll," said Philip. "I imagine that Concordia must be tired and ready to find a camp spot."

"Oh, no," said Concordia. "I could sit here for hours and listen to you guys talk. I'm having the time of my life."

"Well, I'm ready to find a place to crash," said Nathanael. "Wanna go with me, Bashan Boys?"

They agreed, and the group started to break up.

Simon said, "I'm going to look for a sheltered clearing in those bushes up there."

"Okay, Bro," Andrew said. "I'll stay here with Concordia until you get back."

"I'll stay too," said James, "Then I'll go look for my own spot."

John and Philip started up the path toward the prophet's quarters.

"Today was a good day," said John.

"Yeah," said Philip. "Now if the Messiah shows up, things would really be looking good. But I don't think restoring Bashan will be first on his agenda."

"You're right. Hey, I'll show you that scroll I've been working through. I should have time to finish it tomorrow. The prophet doesn't baptize on the Sabbath; it's his only day of rest."

"Good. I'm ready for a day of rest."

7

Priests and Levites

Sunday, 16 March AD 27, 7:00 am

John was greeter at the river today, and Andrew had been sent to be greeter on the Damascus Road. The sun was barely climbing over the low hills above the Damascus Road, and the air was crisp and clean. Two adults had just appeared at the river crossing, and one of them was helping a boy to stand against the river current.

"James! Tad!" John called out.

"Hello!" called back James the Levite. When they reached the shore, Thaddeus greeted John, and James introduced the other man: "John, this is my younger brother Joses."

"Pleased to meet you," said both Joses and John at once.

"James, I didn't know you had a brother," said John.

"Actually, I have two brothers. My older brother is Matthew, but we don't talk about him much. He's a tax collector at Capernaum."

"Oh, I've met Matthew!" John exclaimed. "We have to buy our fishing licenses from him. The bigger our boats, the more it costs. Then we have to pay import and export taxes every time we take fish across the border to and from Bethsaida. Everyone knows he's a Levite. We call him Levi the Taxman."

"Yes, he's the black sheep of the family. When our father died, Matthew demanded his share of the inheritance in cash, and he used the money to buy a position as a tax collector for Herod Antipas. It was a big disgrace for the Alpheus family."

"Well, I'm glad you're here," said John.

"Yes, I'm sorry we're so late. But much has been happening, and I bring important news. The chiefs of Jerusalem are in an uproar, ever since five wealthy men returned from a sight-seeing excursion to hear the prophet. The three rich Pharisees demanded an examination be made of him, and the temple priests have been wondering who this prophet might be. And some among the Levites are wondering if he's trying to start a new religion."

"Oh, why is that?"

"We heard that the baptizer immerses people completely under the water. That's the same thing one does to join our religion. Anyway, they've sent a delegation of priests and Levites to ask the prophet who he is, and they're a few hours behind us. We heard what happened when the five wealthy leaders were here, so Joses and I came ahead to see if we can arrange an audience with the prophet without getting yelled at."

"Wow," mused John. "Prob'ly the best time would be in the afternoon after he's done baptizing. You might want to attend his morning sermon first, and then be baptized if you want to. But he can look in your eyes and see if there is any hidden sin."

"That's not all," said Joses. "The two rich Sadducees sent a messenger to King Herod in Tiberias to tell him what the prophet has been saying about his marriage to Herodias. They're asking that the prophet be put to death. It might get dangerous for the prophet to be here at this location, so near to Herod's territory of Galilee."

"Oh, double wow," responded John. "I'll give that news to the disciples who are closer to the prophet. There's only about seven of them; he sends most people back to their homes."

"Well, I don't think he can start a new religion that way," said Joses.

"Okay, just get together with me after the baptisms, and I'll take you and the delegation to the prophet if they're here by then."

A ten-man group of priests and Levites from Jerusalem arrived about noon, while the baptisms were being completed. The Alpheus family had been among the first to be baptized, and were well dried off. James and Joses joined the delegation and briefed them on the audience that had been arranged, while Thaddeus hung out with John. The Baptist walked over to the group, trailed by a dozen onlookers from the crowd at the river eddy.

One of the priests said, "Greetings! We have been sent from the temple to ask, 'Who are you?'"

"I am not the Messiah," the Baptist said.

"What then, are you Elijah?"

"I am not."

"Are you the prophet like Moses?"

"No."

"Who are you, so we may give an answer to those who sent us? What do you have to say about yourself?

The Baptist was wet, and irritable. He raised his voice: "I AM A VOICE CRYING IN THE WILDERNESS, 'MAKE STRAIGHT THE WAY OF THE LORD!'"

The spokesman was a bit startled, but he went on, "Why then are you baptizing, if you are not the Messiah, nor Elijah, nor the Prophet?"

The Baptist answered saying, "I baptize in water, but among you stands One you do not know. It is he who comes after me, the thong of whose sandal I am not worthy to untie." [26]

Then he turned and walked away, followed by most of his disciples, while the delegation murmured among themselves and the onlookers dispersed.

Andrew, Philip, and Daniel came over to where John and Thaddeus were standing. Philip exclaimed, "Did you hear what the prophet said? He said the 'Greater One' was standing right here among us! Who do you think it might be?"

"I don't know, Philip," said John. "I didn't see anyone who looked really important at all!"

"I think it was the guy with the really beat-up sandals," said Thaddeus.

The others looked at Thaddeus in wonder.

James the Levite came over to them. "Men, we're going back to Jerusalem with them. We want to be part of the discussion when they decide what to do next. Thanks for your help, John. Come on, Thaddeus, we have to go now."

After the young men said their goodbyes, John said, "Daniel, did you guys tell the prophet what the rich Sadducees are trying to do?"

"No, not yet," Daniel said. But he's been looking at us as if he knows it already. The other disciples are telling him right now, back at the house."

"Okay. I'm going to check on my friends down here, and then go up to the house. Today I have to give my report to the prophet about what I found in the scroll I've been reading."

"Well, my son, what you have found?" said the prophet. The other disciples gathered around, including Andrew and Philip.

"I found out a whole lot about what the Essene community at Qumran thinks of itself. They believe they are going to be the righteous 'remnant of Israel,' who will still survive after most everyone else is killed in the Great War."

"Ah, yes, so they do. And?" The prophet left his last word hanging, expectant.

John continued, his voice becoming almost a chant: "Isaiah has written,

> O afflicted one, storm-tossed, and not comforted,
> I am about to set your stones in precious mortar,
> And lay your foundations with sapphires.
> I will make your pillars of rubies,
> Your gates of jewels,
> And your wall of precious stones.[27]

"The author of the *pesher* correctly sees that Isaiah has built a causeway between the twelve precious stones of the chiefs of Israel in Exodus, and Ezekiel's twelve gates of judgment by the chiefs of the tribes. Therefore the interpretation of the word—the *pesher*—is this:

> He will found the council of his assembly,
> Like the sapphire-stone beside the ruby-stone,
> And will raise the pillars of the gates of Jerusalem,
> For judgment by the twelve chiefs of the tribes of Israel."[28]

The room was silent. Andrew was dumbfounded. He had never heard his friend speak as if with the authority of scripture. On the other hand, He had not spent near as much time studying in the synagogue as John had.

The prophet spoke: "Excellent! John, you have graduated. I will teach you no more."

8

THE LAMB OF GOD

MONDAY, 17 MARCH AD 27, 7:00 AM

On the next morning John was standing with Philip, observing the people gather. He was watching for anyone who might be wearing a particularly ragged pair of sandals. He had his own plan on what he was going to do when he found that person.

Andrew joined them and said, "Hey John, I didn't know you were a prophet!"

"Neither did I," said John.

"So what does all that stuff you said mean, anyway?"

"It seems that when the Messiah comes, he will raise up twelve who will be the council of the Messiah's people. Then after the great Day of the Lord, the twelve will sit in judgment on all of Israel."

"Okay, now you're speaking plainly instead of in riddles."

"It will become more plain to you if you will read more scripture."

Later, Philip was helping with baptisms, while Andrew was on the Damascus Road. John was at the water's edge, ushering people to the Baptist and walking them back out of the water.

Suddenly, the prophet looked up from his work, and saw a man walking toward the baptism site. "LOOK!" he called out, "The Lamb of God who takes away the sin of the world!"

The man took notice of the Baptist, but continued walking past the baptism site and toward the river-crossing.

The prophet continued loudly, "This is the One on behalf of whom I said, 'After me comes a man who has a higher rank than I have, for he existed before me.' I did not recognize him, but so that he might be made known to Israel, I came baptizing in water.

"I have seen the Spirit descending as a dove out of heaven, and she remained upon him.[29] I did not recognize him, but he who sent me to baptize in water said to me, 'He upon whom you see the Spirit descending and remaining upon him, this is the One who will baptize in Holy Spirit.' I myself have seen, and I have testified that this is the Son of God."[30]

John was helping an elderly man return to shore, and had no chance to activate his secret plan. Instead, he watched helplessly as the "Son of God"—wearing raggedy sandals—disappeared across the river.

9

MEETING JESUS

TUESDAY, 18 MARCH AD 27, 10:00 AM

The next morning, John and Andrew were walking with the prophet leaving the baptism site, for there had been few people to baptize today. Just then the mysterious man himself came walking vigorously past them, headed toward the Damascus road.

"Look! The Lamb of God!" said the Baptist, as the man passed them by.

John and Andrew left the Baptist and began following the raggedy-sandaled man. He heard them behind him, and turned to see them following. He said, "What's up, guys? What do you seek?"

John and Andrew both started to speak at once, and then stopped. Andrew continued, stammering, "I—uh—Great Teacher, where are you staying?"

The man smiled broadly and said, "Come along, and you will see."

About a half mile up the road, they came to a side trail leading into the bush that John had not noticed before. They followed the man along the trail for a few hundred paces and came to a clearing with five modest houses facing in a semicircle. The mystery man sat down in front of one of the houses, and said, "Well, young men, welcome! Tell me your names."

"I'm Andrew son of Jonah, and this is John, son of Zebedee. We've been staying with the Baptist for almost two weeks."

"Well, I'm Jesus of Nazareth, called the son of Joseph. I've been staying here about a week. The folk that live here call this place *Bet Anaya*, the 'House of the Humble'—or Bethany for short."

"Isn't there a Bethany near Jerusalem?" asked Andrew.

"Yes there is," responded Jesus. "That would make this place Bethany-beyond-Jordan."

John saw that he could belatedly activate his secret plan, and said, "Jesus, I have something for you." He pulled a pair of sandals from inside his clothes. "The Baptist told us if we have two tunics, we should give one to the person who has none. My mom sent these sandals to me just this week, but I already have a pair."

"Thank you, John. By this, you can be certain you will not lose your reward," said Jesus. "The ones I'm wearing look pretty bad, don't they?" Jesus fiddled with the hard-knotted thongs of his old sandals, which were wrapped up and tied around the calves of his legs.

"Here, let me help untie that," said John. Then it flashed on him what the Baptist had said.

"Yes, go ahead," said Jesus.

As a fisherman, John knew knots quite well, and soon had the stiff leather thongs loosened. Then John said, "The Baptist says he is not worthy to untie the thong of your sandal."

Jesus laughed. "Does he not? Then this shows you are more worthy than he, doesn't it?"

John had no answer for that. He asked, "Is it all right if we and our friends stay here tonight?"

"Yes," said Jesus. "Abbaqilah, the master of this house, is generous, and has room to spare."

Andrew said, "Teacher, I'm going to go get my brother and bring him to meet you." And he was off down the trail.

John said, "Teacher, may I go get my brother also?"

Jesus smiled. "What am I to you, young man? We've known one another for less than an hour, and is it time for you to be asking me permission for your comings and goings? Of course you may. I must meet your brother."

John ran after Andrew and caught up with him breathlessly. "Hey, Andrew, do you think we've found the Messiah?"

"Either that or we've been wasting our time hanging out with the Baptist," he said.

"Well, I have a good feeling about this, even if he doesn't act like we expected him to."

They arrived at Simon's campsite, and both Simon and Concordia were there. "Bro, we've found the Messiah!" said Andrew. "He's staying at a house not very far from here."

"Oh, I want to see him!" said Concordia.

"Should we bring all our stuff?" asked Simon.

"I'm sure it'll be okay," said John. "He says there's plenty of room. I'm gonna go find the rest of the guys."

John found his brother James at his campsite, but Philip was nowhere to be found. Nathanael's gear was at his camp under the fig tree, but Nathanael was not there. Daniel said he thought the two of them had gone exploring up the Damascus Road. So the five Galileans started back, and arrived together at "Bethany beyond Jordan." Jesus was outside waiting for them.

Simon and Concordia were at the front of the group. Jesus looked at Simon and said, "You are Simon, the son of Jonah.

You shall be called Cephas, the Stone" (In Greek, his new name would be Peter).[31]

"Come in, all of you! You are expected. The master of the house has prepared a going-away feast for us tonight; we will eat in about an hour."

"Going away?" asked John.

Jesus chuckled. "Yes, that's Abbaqilah's little joke. When new guests arrive he always throws a going-away party on that same day. He gave me my going-away party a week ago."

The food was simple but plentiful, and they got to know and enjoy one another. They found out Jesus had four brothers and three sisters, all of them older than him, and his youngest sister was to be married soon. His mother would be at the wedding, but father Joseph had passed away several years ago. John thought Jesus' story was probably more complex than that, but he reserved his questions for later.

Simon then told about his own story: He grew up in Bethsaida, but was married two months ago and moved to his mother-in-law's big house in Capernaum. Concordia's father died last year, and her mother said the house had been empty for too long. Simon brought his father's fishing boat to Capernaum, but he still partnered with the Zebedee family in the fishing business.

Abbaqilah told how his little community of "humble" folk survived by harvesting and drying figs and nuts that grew naturally near the river, and selling them to caravan merchants bound for Jerusalem. Well-fed and drowsy, they drifted off to sleep one by one.

10

HIT THE ROAD

WEDNESDAY, 19 MARCH AD 27, 6:00 AM

The sun was not quite up yet, but Jesus and John were up early, following the pathway to the house where the Baptist was staying. Jesus had decided to go to Galilee, and was inviting Simon Peter's friends to come with him.

Jesus saw Philip approaching, and they met on the path. Jesus said, "You are Philip son of Jason. I am the one of whom the Baptist spoke. Find your friend Nathanael, and follow me."

"Yes, sir," said Philip. He and John hurried down to find Nathanael, while John briefed Philip on what had happened last night. They found Nathanael still asleep.

"Nathanael! Wake up!" said Philip. "We have found the one written about in the Law and the Prophets—Jesus of Nazareth, the son of Joseph."

Nathanael sat up and blinked. "Nazareth? Can anything good come out of Nazareth?"

"Come and see," Philip said. Nathanael grabbed his stuff, and the three hurried up the road. They caught up to Jesus, who was on his way back to Bethany.

Jesus turned and saw them, and looked at Nathanael. "Look!" he said, "A true Israelite, in whom there is no deceit!"

"How do you know me?" Nathanael said.

Jesus said, "Before Philip called you, when you were under the fig tree, I saw you."

Now when the Baptist had called Nathanael a pillar of Jerusalem, he had been caught speechless. But this time he was ready with a snappy response, and said, "Oh, Great Teacher! You are the Son of God! You are the King of Israel!" But immediately he was sorry he said it.

Jesus burst out laughing, his sides shaking. When he had composed himself, he went along with Nathanael's joke, saying, "Ah, because I said to you that I saw you under the fig tree, do you now believe? You will see greater things than these!"

Then he switched to a serious tone. He said, "In truth I say to all of you, you will see the heavens opened and the angels of God ascending and descending on the *Son of Adam*." [32]

When they got back to Bethany, the rest of the group was packing up for travel. Abbaqilah brought some bread sweetened with honey to send them on their way. "Here's your last course for the going-away feast," he said.

Jesus said, "Thank you, Abbaqilah, and may peace rest upon your house and family. Goodbye for now."

John asked Jesus, "Where are we going, Teacher?"

Jesus said, "We are bound for Cana in Galilee, and we have no time to waste."

Then he added, "You are all invited to the wedding feast."

11

A Wedding at Cana

Friday, 21 March ad 27, 11:00 am

On the third day, they reached the town of Cana.

The guests for the wedding were already arriving, and the festivities were about to begin. A dozen or more children outside were running around shouting and laughing, playing a game with a hoop made of willow, rolling it along with sticks. That was one of John's favorite games, and he longed to join in. But he was afraid his friends would see him playing like a little kid and make fun of him, so he followed the others to the big house of Maimon, the father of the groom.

They were greeted at the door by a smiling woman. "Hi, I'm Mary, Jesus' mother. Welcome! Who's going to introduce me to all of you?"

Jesus embraced his mother. "Mother, these folks are interested in what my Father in heaven has called me to do, and we're spending some time getting to know each other." Then he began introducing each one by name, beginning with Simon Peter and ending with Nathanael.

Mary said, "I've seen you before, Nathanael, when I was in Cana last year with Anna for her betrothal ceremony. Your whole family has been invited to the wedding!"

Nathanael said, "I'm pleased to meet you, Mary. So Anna is your daughter?"

"Yes she is. Her birth mother died in childbirth, and I married her father Joseph a year later. I've been taking care of her since she was a little baby, and now she's finally getting married!"

"Why do you say 'finally,' Mary"?

"She had a tragic time for quite a while. She was betrothed to be married to a young man eleven years ago, but her fiancé got caught up in a rebellion against the Romans, and was killed in a sword battle. It took a long time for peace to come back into her life."

"I'm sorry to hear that. But now by God's will her time of joy has come," said Nathanael.

"I'm so happy for her, Mary," said Concordia. "This will truly be a joyous time. Simon and I were married a little more than two months ago, and we are very happy. You should come down and visit me and my mother in Capernaum. It's only one long day's journey from here."

"I would love to, Concordia, but I'm travelling with the four sons of Father Joseph, and I'll probably return to Nazareth with them when they go back after the wedding."

"Who knows? Maybe they'd like to visit us also. Have they been to Cana before?"

"Yes, especially Joseph Junior, the second oldest. He's been spending time here with Anna's fiancé, working with him to build a new house for the couple to move into. They are excited about what they have been able to accomplish. Everything is ready now."

The two women continued talking, drifting over to the food preparation area where a dozen young women were helping a servant girl prepare delicacies. But mostly they were talking excitedly.

The group with Jesus drifted into a larger room, where more men of all ages—15 to 55—were gathered, talking energetically. John was still not yet 14, but he tried to blend in.

Later the Rabbi of the synagogue arrived, along with many of the white-bearded elders of the town. Before long a short ceremony was held outside, and the guests cheered and congratulated the happy couple while a small band of musicians struck up a joyous tune.

The guests broke into song and formed a circle dance around the couple, clasping each other side by side around the waist, in two circles, one within the other. Everyone joined in: young, old, adults, children, and even the more spry among the elders, stepping and hopping and skipping and laughing as they joyfully danced round and round.

John was exhilarated; finally he was having some fun. It seemed like the dance would last forever. But when the musicians took a break between tunes, someone announced that the food was ready inside.

And ready it was, with a huge spread laid out on a long table: meats and cheeses and vegetables and sweetbreads and wine. John ate his fill, and then ate again.

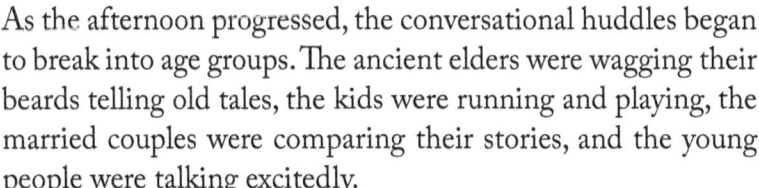

As the afternoon progressed, the conversational huddles began to break into age groups. The ancient elders were wagging their beards telling old tales, the kids were running and playing, the married couples were comparing their stories, and the young people were talking excitedly.

Philip and Nathanael and John's brother James were in the midst of a cluster of young men and women laughing and talking, drinking wine, and telling jokes. Andrew was over in a corner chatting with two young women, and John saw when one of them leaned over to whisper something in Andrew's ear. Andrew blushed as red as a beet.

John was overfull and had a bit of a headache from the wine. Most of the people here in Cana were strangers to him, and he hadn't found anyone his age to talk to. He found a quiet side room that held wineskins on a shelf and led out to a patio with a fig tree at its center. John sat down in a corner of the room and nibbled on a piece of sweetbread with cheese.

John's eyes dropped closed for a minute, but he opened them again when he heard people moving about. Two of the household servants had come into the room, followed by Jesus' mother and Jesus himself. One of the servants gave a small wineskin to Mary. She said, "This is the last one? Jesus, they have run out of wine!"

Jesus was perplexed. He said, "Woman, what does that have to do with you or with me? My time has not yet come."

Mary looked at Jesus. Then she looked at the servants. Then she said to them, "Do whatever he tells you to do," and left the room carrying the small wineskin.

Now next to the outside door there were six large stone waterpots which could hold 20 to 30 gallons of water each, to be used for ritual cleansing. Jesus said to the servants, "Fill all these waterpots with water." Then he went back to rejoin the celebration.

Maimon's patio looked over the town square where there was a water well. John watched as the servants carried buckets of water from the well into the house. By the time they had finished, Jesus returned and told them, "Now draw some out and take it to the ruler of the feast."

Jesus left the servants to their task, but John's curiosity was aroused by these strange events. He followed the servants to the main banquet room, where Jesus' oldest brother James—

who they called James the Just—was at the head of the table, seated near Simon Peter. Receiving a cup from the servants, James tasted the water—which had now changed to wine—and called the bridegroom over to his side.

James said to him, "Everyone else serves the good wine first, then when the guests have drunk deeply they bring out the lesser wine. But you've kept the best wine until last!" John was amazed. He sat down with his cup near Simon to get a taste of this waterpot wine.[33]

Simon Peter said to James, "So you are the oldest son of Joseph?"

"Yes, there are four of us," he said. "Father Joseph was a construction worker, skilled in working with wood and stone and bricks and mortar. He built many houses. Joseph Junior, the second son, loves construction work and took over the business of our father. The two younger sons are Simon and Jude, and they love to work with the soil. Our family owns thirty acres of farmland just a mile west of Nazareth, and they sow and harvest crops out there. All three of them have built their own houses in Nazareth, but I still live in my father's house along with Mary and her son Jesus."

Peter continued, "So how did you come to be called 'James the Just'?"

"Oh, I've been active working with the council of the town's elders, and they've put me in charge of the distribution of food to the orphans and widows," James said.

John noticed the peculiar way in which James referred to his brother Jesus, but thought it might be rude to ask him about that. He resolved to ask someone else about it later.

Later that night, the bride and bridegroom retired to their newly built home, while the local wedding guests went back to their homes in town and the guests from out-of-town found rooms to retire to in Maimon's house. John sought out his friends, finding Andrew and Philip and Nathanael and his brother James. James was asleep already, having drunk a bit too much wine, but the other three were talking quietly.

John said, "Hi guys. Hey Andrew, do you remember when you said we might have been wasting our time hanging around with the Baptist?"

"Yeah, why?" responded Andrew.

"I don't think we wasted our time. Wait'll I tell you what I saw today!"

John told them the story of how Jesus had changed water into wine, and said, "There's still more than a hundred gallons of wine in the supply room! The master of the house is going to be really surprised. He won't know what to do with it."

Philip said, "I never heard of any magician or sorcerer who could do anything like that. How could this happen?"

Nathanael said, "God must be with this guy Jesus, or he would not be able do this."

12

EARLY MORNING WITH JESUS

SATURDAY, 22 MARCH AD 27, 6:00 AM

John was up early, sitting under a tree just outside of town with many things to think about. This had been a busy and astonishing week: Nathanael brought John's brother and fishing friends to see the Baptist, James the Levite brought his own family from Ephraim, priests and Levites came questioning from Jerusalem, he himself made his report about the scroll, and a really ordinary-looking man—Jesus of Nazareth—was identified as the Messiah. Then Jesus invited all of them to a "going-away" feast and then to a marriage feast three day's journey away.

But now, John was about to return to Capernaum and to his own home in Bethsaida, where he would face his father Zebedee again. He remembered painfully his father telling him how disappointed he had been in his youngest son. John was responsible for losing their most valuable fishing net and almost losing the family fishing boat, not to mention his own life and that of his friends. He remembered apologizing, but still wished he could do more.

"Good morning, John."

Even though the voice was unexpected, John was not startled. It was Jesus.

"Oh, good morning, Teacher."

Jesus sat down beside John, and said, "I like the early morning. I spend the time with my Father in heaven praying. But sometimes I just sing to the Lord."

"I like mornings too. It's peaceful. I was just thinking about my father in Bethsaida."

"Is there something troubling you?"

"Yes, a little," John said. "I was thinking again about sinking my father's boat. But I already told you the story of what happened."

"But there is more, isn't there?" responded Jesus.

"Yes. I brought disgrace on my family. My father was embarrassed to ask the townspeople to help salvage the boat, and he was ashamed of me. I repaid my father for the damage I did, but I'm sure he feels he has lost honor in the town. He is a very proud man. I admitted my guilt in the temple and made a guilt offering, then I admitted my guilt to the Baptist and was baptized as a sign of repentance—but I still feel ashamed."

"I know just what you are feeling, John, for I experienced the same thing," said Jesus.

John said wonderingly, "No, not you?"

"Yes, me. When I was twelve years old and visiting Jerusalem for the Passover feast, I stayed behind in the temple, even though I knew my family was returning to Nazareth with the rest of the people from our town. When I was missed, Joseph and my mother had to return a whole day's journey back to Jerusalem to find me, and some of the other townsfolk went with them to help search for me."[34]

"Oh, wow. So then you brought disgrace on your family like I did, and caused your father to lose honor in Nazareth," said John in awe.

"Yes I did. I thought it was time for me to start working with my Father in heaven to fulfill the prophecies spoken over me. But that time had not yet been fulfilled. Instead it was time for me to remain in subjection to my family. I needed to wait, and grow taller and wiser before going on to do more."

"I'll bet you were in a lot of trouble."

"Yes," said Jesus. "I hadn't yet been made a son of the law, so father Joseph bore my sin for me and had to make atonement for my action. He made a guilt offering in the temple and confessed that he had not instructed me correctly and had not supervised me properly."

"Oh, I bet that was tough to hear," responded John.

"Oh yes, and father Joseph took me with him to the altar to make sure I heard it."

"Did you feel bad for a long time?"

"Yes, John, but I was comforted that my Father in heaven counted me innocent and that he had forgiven father Joseph, who confessed his guilt and repented from it.

"John, you may be sure that the Father in heaven has forgiven you also, and that all is well in your relationship with him. But as you have found out, there are other consequences for sin. You will have to pay those consequences, and your family will also suffer the consequences."

John said, "But then what am I supposed to do?"

"The Baptist has the answer to that. Have you not been listening to what he preaches?"

"Um, yes. But what part do you mean?"

"The Baptist tells everyone, 'Bear fruit in keeping with repentance.' That is the key to healing. It will heal your own hurt, and will heal others you have hurt. When your father sees you leading a life of responsibility and integrity, he will forget his hurt. But it will take much time."

"Thank you, Jesus."

"One more thing, John."

"Yes, Teacher?"

"I learned a lesson from my Father in heaven when I tried to fulfill my calling so soon, and the Father has the same lesson for you."

"Oh, yes, what is it, Teacher?"

"King David's son Solomon wrote, 'There is an appointed time for everything under the heavens.'[35] The father in Heaven appoints these times according to his own counsel. He has appointed a time when I must reveal myself and my message to Israel. He has also appointed a time for you, John, to go fishing without your father Zebedee. That time has not come yet, but when it does, you will be fishing for a different quarry, and using a different net."

The afternoon had brought warm sunshine, with just a hint of spring in the air. John was passing through the patio of the big house, just as the sun was getting ready to slip over the horizon. On the fig tree the tips of the dead-looking, twig-like branches had long since turned supple, green, and fuzzy, and now their tiny leaf buds were beginning to spread out into great soft leaves, larger than a man's hand.

Anna's two older sisters, Mary and Salome, came out into the patio with their husbands behind them, followed by Mary the mother of Jesus. The elder Mary said, "Now you two keep warm; it's going to be after dark before you get to the city limits of Sepphoris."

"Oh, mom, we're going to be fine," said the younger Mary.

"We won't be wasting any time," added Salome. "And we've got these two big hunks of men here to keep us safe. Besides, I'll be glad to get back to the city. It seems like forever since I've lived in a tiny town like this one."

Jesus' mother said, "Simon Peter has invited me and all your brothers to visit him down in Capernaum, and we'll be leaving first thing in the morning. He says he has a nice house looking over the lake. I'm not that anxious to get back to Nazareth, now that all you girls have moved out. Think of that! Wanderlust, at my age!"

"Goodbye!" "Goodbye mom," they said.

"May God protect you all. Goodbye."

"So John," Mary asked, "how are you doing? Are you excited to be going home tomorrow?"

"Yes, ma'am, sort of. I've been gone almost a month—that's the longest I've ever been away from home," said John.

"Well, I've been happy to spend this time with my stepdaughters. I miss them, and I'm going to miss living with Anna."

John saw a chance to clear up some oddities that were on his mind, and screwed up his courage to ask, "Ma'am, may I ask you a question?"

Mary laughed. "Of course you may, John. If I'm in a good mood, maybe I'll even answer you!"

John felt put at ease a little. "I heard James talking about his three brothers and 'Jesus son of Mary.' Are all five of them brothers or not?"

"Oh, let me sit down here and tell you all about it. Part of it is simple, and part of it is very mysterious. First of all, father Joseph adopted Jesus, so he's just as much a part of the family as the other four. I don't know why James still talks like that. When I married Joseph, James was around your age, and I was only a couple years older than him. I got along with the girls really well, but it took some time before the boys accepted me as their new mother.

"But here's the mysterious part: After I was betrothed to Joseph, and before we were married, an angel of God appeared to me, and told me I was going to be overshadowed by the Holy Spirit, and conceive a boy in my womb—without ever having been with a man! When Joseph found out, he was disturbed. But an angel of God appeared to him in a dream, and told him to name the boy Jesus, because he would save his people from their sins."

"Wow," John said quietly. "Jesus told me there'd been prophecies spoken over him when he was a child."

"Yes, shepherds and travelers from far away visited us after he was born, saying that the baby would be the Anointed One, the King of Israel. And there were two prophets in the temple who said this baby would be the redemption of Israel, and a light of revelation to the peoples of the world."

"This is not going to make Emperor Tiberius very happy in Rome," speculated John.

"It didn't make King Herod the Great very happy in Jerusalem when he got wind of it from the travelers. Joseph was warned in a dream, and we ran away to Egypt with the whole family and stayed for four years, until Herod died. I heard that Herod killed a lot of babies to try to assassinate the new Anointed One." [36]

"So what's going to happen next, Mary?"

"I don't know. I don't know if Jesus knows. He has had a faraway look in his eyes since he came back from being baptized in the Jordan. I think he spent more than a month in the desert after that." [37]

"He sure made an impression on John the Baptist. The Baptist also prophesied about Jesus, and said that he was the Son of God."

"Yes, that was John son of Zechariah. Did you know he is the second cousin of Jesus?"

John exclaimed, "No I didn't! The Baptist said he didn't recognize him!"

"Perhaps he meant he didn't recognize that Jesus was the Anointed One. But they haven't seen each other since they were small children. John is the son of my cousin Elizabeth, who has passed away to a blessed rest in the bosom of Abraham."

"Well, you're sure right about one thing, ma'am: this is really mysterious. But Jesus told me nothing will happen until the right time comes—the time set by our Father in heaven."

"Yes, John, I pray every morning and every night for the Lord to show us the way forward."

"That's what I need to do—pray more. I'm gonna try doing it the way Jesus does."

Suddenly Nathanael burst into the patio from the house, trailed by his cousin Matthias. "Hey, there you are, John," he said. "I came to let you know I'm not going with you guys to Capernaum right now. Matthias and I need to travel to Caesarea to buy more supplies from the wool markets. The family's spinning wheels are empty, and the rug looms will soon be going hungry unless we buy something to feed them." He chuckled at his lame joke. "We're leaving now and we'll spend the night in Sepphoris before going on to Caesarea."

"Boys, if you hurry you can catch up to my girls and their husbands," mother Mary said. "I'm sure they'll be glad to give you a place to sleep tonight."

"Oh, thanks for the tip," said Nathanael. "Goodbye, Ma'am. See you later, John. Maybe we'll see each other at the Passover feast in Jerusalem next month."

"Okay Nate," John said. Then he tried his own lame joke: "Don't try to spend any of those woolen shekels in your pocket."

13

Capernaum and Family

Sunday, 23 March AD 27, 5:00 pm

There were 12 in the travel party: John and James sons of Zebedee; Concordia with Simon and Andrew sons of Jonah; James, Joseph, Simon, and Jude sons of Joseph; Philip; and Mary with Jesus. They had made good time, and were in sight of Capernaum an hour before sunset. [38]

They had taken the well-paved Roman road from Cana to the new lakeside city of Tiberias. With its long wall and grand synagogue, it had been built by Herod Antipas to honor the emperor. However, Herod had built the city over an ancient cemetery, and most Jews would not enter through the city gates, for the cemetery made it ritually unclean. The synagogue was sitting empty, while Herod was looking for foreigners to populate his new city.

Following the lakeshore of the Sea of Galilee, the twelve passed the fish processing town of Magdala and the farms on the Plain of Kinnereth, and were nearing their journey's end.

A distant voice boomed from across the lake: "Ahoy!"

John got excited. "It's Dad!" John called back, "Ahoy!" but his voice was swallowed up by the lapping of the waves at the lakeshore.

"I see him! Over there to the left," James Zebedee said, and pointed to a faint blip across the waters, caught in the gleam of the afternoon sun.

"Nobody can yell like my dad can yell," said John, to anyone who cared to hear.

"He does measure up to your stories about him," said Jesus.

"It looks like he has a full crew in the boat," Andrew said. "They look to be pulling toward Capernaum. They'll probably beat us there."

It had been a long day, but they quickened their pace as they approached the first lakeside houses of the unwalled town of Capernaum. They reached the center of town just as the rugged old fisherman Zebedee steered his boat to the water's edge, with his long-time servants Samuel and Sheva and the two Bashan brothers at the oars.

Simon Peter called out, "Hey, Zebedee, catch anything?"

"Yes," he boomed, "My death of cold. And a few minnows." He sneezed, then wiped his nose with a cloth.

Simon introduced the visitors to Zebedee and his crew, including "Jesus of Nazareth, son of Joseph," and said, "Jesus has given me a new name, Cephas the stone. But I like it in Greek better: Simon Peter."

Jesus stepped forward and shook Zebedee's hand, saying, "Pleased to meet you, father. You have raised some fine sons here."

Zebedee said, "Yes, we're from good cheerful Bhagavan stock. But I've been searching the family genealogy lately for a trace of any swashbuckling Tookiy[39] lineage. I didn't know we had burglar blood in us!" He laughed at his own joke, taken at John's expense. John winced.

Jesus also laughed at the joke, and placed a hand on Zebedee's shoulder. "Fear not for them, Zebedee, for they'll be slaying dragons before long. And be healed of your sickness, and strengthened for your journey home."

Zebedee said, "Thank you for the blessing. I feel better already."

Concordia joined in, saying, "Why don't you and your crew come up to the house for some hot tea from India and a bite to eat? It will pep you up a bit."

Zebedee glanced at Simon Peter, then said, "Don't mind if I do."

They headed for Concordia's family home, on a low bluff just a couple hundred yards from the beach. John and the Bashan brothers brought up the rear of the entourage, now up to 17 people.

Beon said, "Zebedee was dropping us at home here, then he was gonna sail to Bethsaida in front of this nice westerly breeze. You and James gonna go with him?"

"Yes, probably," John said. "I've been away from home quite a while now."

"I don't suppose that this Jesus fellow is the Baptist's 'Messiah,' is he?"

"Yes, I think so. I saw a sign of his power when we were in Cana."

Bohan said, "I hope he's got a bigger army than this group. The Romans will chew him and his 'army' up into little pieces."

"Maybe a time will come when he doesn't need an army, if God is with him," John said.

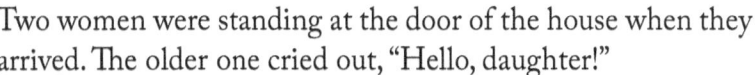

Two women were standing at the door of the house when they arrived. The older one cried out, "Hello, daughter!"

"Hello, Mom!" said Concordia. "Folks, this is my mom Perpetua, and our servant Mina. Mom, I've brought a whole army to you for a cup of tea!"

"Oh, don't worry, child. We saw you coming even before Zebedee arrived. The water's already on the fire, and we've got lots of fresh bread that Mina and I baked just today. Welcome, all of you! Come in!"

Simon Peter again took the job to introduce all the newcomers to Perpetua. Her home was warm and spacious. Mary thought it looked too large for two women to take care of, maybe even for three. She said, "Perpetua, Are you three women and Simon the only ones living here?"

"Yes, Mary," she said, "except that Andrew and Philip sleep here during fishing season to help Simon. My other four daughters are all married and gone now. My husband's father was the Lord Mayor for Herod the Great and had several servants, but they all passed on before my husband died. I never had a son to inherit the place. It's a blessing to have Simon move in with us; he's the son I never had."

Philip found John to update him on travel plans: "Hey, John, Andrew and I are gonna stay here tonight. My rowboat is beached here in Capernaum, so you can look for us in Bethsaida tomorrow sometime. If you see his parents or my parents, tell them we're coming."

14

A WALK ON THE BEACH

Thursday, 27 March AD 27, 9:00 am

The last three days had been busy for Zebedee's fishing crew. They were searching for the big school of prime fish he knew was out there; it was just a matter of finding it. But the winds had been calm, so John and James and Samuel and Sheva had been doing a lot of heavy rowing. Finally they had run across a respectable school of fish. They weren't the prime variety Zebedee was looking for—the ones that brought high prices in Jerusalem—but they were still salable to non-Jews. They hauled in thirty fish with their throw-net, and took them to Bethsaida to sell to the new non-Jewish processing plant there.

Today they were on their way across the lake to Capernaum, carrying extra passengers. John's mother Salome wanted to visit Perpetua, and "see this man Jesus." Andrew was on board, and Philip had brought his father Jason. Simon Peter was at the shoreline to greet them.

Peter called out, "Yo, Andrew! It's about time you got here! The fish are waiting for us!"

"I dunno, bro," said Andrew. "They've been hiding out from the Zebedee crew."

Peter helped them beach the boat, and Zebedee helped his wife disembark and get to shore. Salome said, "Hello, Simon, how's your wife? And how's Perpetua?"

"Oh, they're doing great, Salome. How have you been? And what about Zebedee here? I thought he had the sniffles."

"Yes he did, and he was miserable. But then your man Jesus laid a hand on him, and his sniffles were gone, like a snap of the fingers. I don't know what to think about that."

"Well, come on up to the house and meet him! See for yourself what you think. You'll have a chance to meet his mother and his brothers. They're leaving for Nazareth tomorrow, so they can get ready to go to Jerusalem for Passover."

Andrew asked, "What's Jesus planning to do, Bro?"

"I'm not sure," Simon said. "But he's not going back to Nazareth with his brothers."

The afternoon was upon them, and Perpetua was still talking earnestly with Salome and Concordia, while the men were listening to the brothers of Jesus tell childhood stories of their four-year stay in Egypt. But Simon Peter sought out John and Andrew and said, "The teacher is outside and wants to talk with us. Find Philip and James and come out."

Jesus smiled at the five men. "Children, let's take a walk along the beach." The afternoons had begun to warm up under the growing warmth of the spring sun, and a pleasant westerly breeze was blowing.

Jesus began to speak as they walked. "You've all heard John the Baptist preach that the kingdom of God is at hand.

The time of preparation has come upon Israel, and he is in the wilderness calling for men and women to make ready for what will come next; to repent, with a visible sign of their repentance, and to bear fruit worthy of repentance.

"You know great things are near to us. The Father has sent each of you to me because you will each play a part in what is to come. The parts you will play haven't been revealed to you, but you'll learn that a little at a time.

"As I have taught you, the time is not yet fulfilled for me to reveal myself and my mission to all of Israel. While this time of the Baptist is upon us, I will preach the message of the Baptist—the message that he received from my Father in heaven.

"I must go to Jerusalem for Passover, and I'll remain in Judea afterwards, preaching preparation for the kingdom. I will need workers when I start, and the Father will send me other workers while I am there. It would be best if you men will work with me after Passover for a while. Do you have any questions?"

John asked, "When are we leaving?"

Jesus laughed. "Ah, eager to go, are you? No, we will not all leave together. Go to Jerusalem with your families and your friends, and meet me in the Lower City after Passover. Now leave me and go back to the house, while I have a few more words with this eager disciple."

John knew that meant him, and he wondered what was on Jesus' mind. The two of them continued to walk down the beach as the other four men turned back.

"John, you have seen the scribes and sages teaching their disciples, have you not?"

"Yes, Teacher, in Jerusalem, and often on the Temple Mount."

"How many disciples do they usually teach?"

"It's a Pharisee custom that they each have five disciples, but some have more."

"And if they have rank among themselves, who seems to have the lowest rank?"

"Sometimes the newest one, but usually it's the youngest."

"Ah, John, you know quite a bit. You are observant. So have you noticed what are the duties of the lowest disciple?"

"Yes. The lowest-ranking disciple takes care of the personal needs of the teacher, such as fetching his water, or untying his sandals. He is always at the teacher's side."

"Yes, John, and that's the task you will bear. You will be the least of my disciples, the one of lowest rank. Even if there is a younger disciple, you will remain as the least. Other disciples will write about me, but you will be the last to write. But you will be by my side at times when no one else is with me, and you will see things no other disciple will see."

"Oh."

"But there is more, for when the kingdom of God comes, the first will become the last, and the last will become first. Are you ready for this task?"

"Yes."

"I am leaving for Jerusalem in three days, and I want you to come with me," Jesus said. Then he added, "I must meet your friend Hezekiah."

15

CITY OF DAVID

THURSDAY, 3 APRIL AD 27, 12:00 NOON

"Hezzy! Hello!"

John had just spotted his friend down a winding back alley of the City of David, after following directions from other street kids who knew him. Most buildings here were one-room mud huts with flat roofs, often with ladders or exterior stairs leading up to the roof. Here and there some of the houses had an upper room with a small window or two.

Hezekiah came running, talking excitedly: "John! This is great! Did you see the prophet? What's he like? What's he say?"

John couldn't help but laugh. "Yes I did, Hezzy, and I stayed with him almost two weeks. He's actually a nice guy. But he was prophesying 'bout a greater man that would come after him, and guess what?"

"Oh, what?"

"The greater man came, and I met him! He's Jesus of Nazareth, and he's coming here!" [40]

"What, here? No! Is he the Messiah?"

"That hasn't been revealed yet. He wants me to call him the Teacher of Israel for now. He wants to meet you, Hezekiah."

"WHAT? No! He's coming HERE?"

John laughed again. "Yup, that's what I said. Which house is yours, Hezzy?"

"You just passed it. We have a spare room upstairs, but it doesn't really have a roof on it, just a few palm fronds. HERE? NOW? Wait, I gotta go clean it up! Me and my friends have been playing up there. It's our play fort, where we defend Jerusalem against the Romans."

"No, no, wait, Hezzy! Go tell your mom, and see if it's all right. Then I'll go get Jesus, and we'll be back in an hour, if we have your mom's permission."

"Oh it'll be okay, I'm sure! I'll tell my mom he's gonna pay one lepton a day for rent."

"Okay Hezzy, and you don't need to worry about food, we've got some with us."

When Jesus and John arrived at Hezekiah's house, the whole family was standing outside the door to greet them, with the children lined up beside their mother, and a baby in her arms.

John said, "Hezekiah, this is Jesus of Nazareth."

Hezekiah said, "Welcome, great Teacher. We are honored by your visit. My father Malchiel is no longer with us. This is my mother Abigail. My brother David is seven years old, and Dan is six. My sister Rebekah is four, and Rachel is two. And baby Deborah is six months old."

Jesus said, "Thank you, young man. And I am pleased to meet you, mother Abigail. How is your baby, is she well?"

"No sir," said Abigail, "I am worried about her; she has a fever and seems to be getting weaker."

"Do not fear for your daughter, Abigail. She will become healthy and strong. May I hold her?"

Jesus took the baby and held her in his arms. He said, "Hezekiah, I have come to celebrate the Passover with you and your family. The Lord himself will provide the Passover lamb for the sacrifice, and together we will eat it with your family." Jesus then talked with each of the other children, and then gave the baby back to Abigail.

"Oh!" exclaimed Abigail, "Her fever is gone! Thank you, sir."

Jesus and John stowed their packs in the upper room, which had been tidied and swept. There was a small window overlooking the alley, and a thin sleeping pallet along one wall. "I hope we aren't taking someone's pallet," said John to Hezekiah.

"Oh, no," he said, "That's my father's pallet. No one has slept on it since he left."

"We will care for it well," said Jesus.

Jesus and John went down and sat on the bottom of the stairway, where Jesus wanted to rest and watch the foot traffic in the alley. Hezekiah ran off to find his friends and tell them what was happening at his house.

Less than an hour later, a woman came down the alley carrying an infant, and approached Jesus. "Great Sir, would you hold my baby? She is unwell and needs a blessing."

Jesus asked the woman what her baby's name was, and held the baby in his arms for a few minutes. When he gave the baby back, the mother's face lit up with a smile and she thanked him. Before long there was a small crowd of young mothers in the alley who were bringing their sick babies for Jesus to hold. Jesus held each one and healed every one of them.

Then a middle-aged man and his son appeared from up the alleyway, carrying a large wooden chair and some cushions. It was a sturdy armchair made entirely of hardwood. They approached Jesus, and the man said, "Great Teacher, I have brought a chair for you to sit in. This is the throne of King David. I made it myself, and it is yours to sit in any time you visit David's city."

"Thank you," Jesus said. "You have done fine work. I am a carpenter myself, and I appreciate those who know well how to work with wood."

Just before sundown, in spite of John's protestations, Abigail invited Jesus and John inside the house for a meal. She served them flatbread and a tasty lentil soup. They ate alongside the whole family, while Abigail nursed her baby girl, who was vigorous and hungry.

16

A TALK WITH THE RABBI

SATURDAY, 5 APRIL AD 27, 7:00 AM

"Rabbi Yanai? This is Jesus of Nazareth," Hezekiah said. He and his brother David and John and Jesus had found the rabbi at the back of the Synagogue of David.

"Ah, yes, Jesus of Nazareth! I'm glad to meet you. Many are talking about you. They tell me that men and women from all over the City of David have been coming to you to be healed of their sickness."

"My Father is working, and I also must work," said Jesus.

"And I am also told you are staying with the widow Abigail. Are you a kinsman of hers?"

"Yes, a kinsman, for I am a *son of Adam*. But I am not a close kin."

"That is a pity. She has no close kin to watch over her, and her children have no father to teach them the law of Moses. I have been working with young Hezekiah, who is an excellent student. He knows much about our law, and some about our customs as well. But if I present him to the synagogue as a son of the law, he will become the head of his household, and counted responsible for the misdeeds of his brothers and sisters. He is not yet ready for that burden."

"He is in good hands with you, Rabbi," Jesus said. "God is blessing the work you are doing. Hezekiah's mother has been unable to celebrate Passover for two years now, because she has been unable to buy a lamb for the sacrifice, and her neighbors are suffering likewise. But we will celebrate this year, and Hezekiah will be at the head of the table for the Passover feast."

"Ah, very good. He knows the responses for the Passover feast, don't you, Hezekiah? Tell me, Hezekiah, how does one fulfill his duty on Passover night?"

Hezekiah said, "You do not fulfill your duty on Passover night unless you mention three things: the Passover lamb—because the angel of death passed over the houses of the fathers in Egypt; and unleavened bread—because the fathers had been set free from Egypt; and bitter herbs—because life under the Egyptians was bitter."

"Very good! Did I not tell you, Jesus? But now, Hezekiah, you must teach your brother David the three questions to ask. And Jesus, while you are here, will you read the Haftarah?"

When it was time for the service, the synagogue was packed shoulder to shoulder, for Jerusalem was filling up with people from far and near for Passover. John and his two friends stood at a vantage point by Jesus' chair. When the time came for the reading from Moses, the room was too full to parade the scroll around the room, so the rabbi stood up from his chair and began to read:

Moses called for all the leaders of Israel in Egypt and said to them, "Each of you must choose a lamb or a young goat and kill it, so that your families can celebrate Passover. Take a sprig of hyssop, dip it in the animal's blood, and wipe the blood on the doorposts and beam above the door of your house. Not one of you is to leave the house until morning. When the Lord goes through Egypt to slay the Egyptians, he will see the blood on the doorposts and the beam and will not let the angel of death enter your houses to kill you.

"When you enter the Promised Land, you must perform this ritual: When your children ask you, 'What does this ritual mean?' you will answer, 'It is the sacrifice of Passover to honor the Lord, because he passed over the houses of Israel in Egypt. He killed the Egyptians, but he spared us.' You and your children must obey these rules forever." [41]

The whole congregation sang a familiar psalm, then the Rabbi spoke. "This is Jesus of Nazareth. He will read the Haftarah to us." The scroll of Isaiah was handed to Jesus, and he stood up and began to read:

> The servant of the Lord was treated cruelly, but endured it humbly; he never said a word.
> Like a lamb about to be slaughtered, like a sheep about to be sheared, he never said a word.
> He was arrested and sentenced and led off to die, and no one cared about his fate.
> He was put to death for the sins of our people.
> He was placed in a grave with those who are evil; he was buried with the rich, even though he had never committed a crime or ever told a lie.[42]

Jesus sat down and was silent for a moment.

Then he said, "Oh, Jerusalem, Jerusalem, how you have killed the prophets! And how you will yet kill the coming Lamb of God! Woe to you, Jerusalem! You make fine tombs for the prophets and for those who lead good lives; and you claim that if you had lived during the time of your ancestors, you would not have done what they did and killed the prophets. So you admit you are the descendants of those who killed the prophets!

"Go on, then, and finish the job your ancestors started! For I tell you now that my Father is sending you the Lamb of God, but you will not listen to him, and you will kill him. Repent now, while there is yet time! Show forth fruits of your repentance, for there will be no hope for those who do not repent."[43]

17

Lambs Aplenty

Wednesday, 9 April AD 27, 12:00 noon

"John! David! Come Quick! Look!" Hezekiah was excited. David and Dan appeared at their front door, while John came down the stairs. "Look! Sheep!"

At the end of the alley, a herd of sheep had appeared. There seemed to be four men driving them up the alley, and two sheep dogs keeping them together in a bunch. Jesus followed John down the stairs. "Thank you, Father," Jesus said. Abigail appeared at her door with her girls.

Jesus recognized two of the sheep drivers: they were his brothers James and Joseph. He called out, "James! Joseph! Welcome! What brings you to Mount Zion?"

The brothers waved at Jesus, and continued driving the sheep until the whole herd was bunched in the alley with Hezekiah's house at the center of them. Every one of them was a young male sheep—a lamb. With Jesus' brothers were two shepherds, who were evidently the owners of the two sheep dogs. Street children were gathering to look at this strange sight.

"Hello, Jesus!" said James. "They told us we would find you here."

Jesus said, "So tell us all the story of how you happen to be here with a herd of sheep."

Joseph said, "It was the strangest thing. I had a dream a week ago. An angel of God appeared to me in the dream and said, 'The City of David has no lambs and cannot celebrate the Passover. They cannot pay the prices being charged for lambs at the Temple. Who will bring lambs to David's city?' So I went and asked James what we should do, and he said we must bring the lambs ourselves."

James continued the story: "We found only four male lambs left in Nazareth, for no flocks of sheep were in the area. So we came ahead of the rest of the family, driving the four lambs. But as we travelled, people came from the villages and found what we were doing, and each village that we passed in Galilee and Judea contributed at least one lamb. These two good shepherds here gave two lambs and came to help us, for we had too many sheep to handle by ourselves. We ended up with 40 lambs altogether!"

Joseph picked it up from there. "We just came from the Sheep Gate, where we presented these lambs to the priests for inspection. Not one of the lambs has a blemish! But of course, we had to pay the customary bribe for each lamb that was inspected."

Then James picked it up. "But we cannot just give the lambs away, for no one can sacrifice a lamb which he has not paid for. We will need at least 40 lepta for this herd of lambs."

Hezekiah, who had been listening raptly, burst out, "Oh! I will buy them! I have 40 lepta!"

Abigail asked, "Hezekiah, where did you get 40 lepta?"

"I've been saving up for a tunic, mom. The coins are buried in the corner where I sleep. Just think, mom, I can sell the lambs for 40 shekels at least!"

Jesus said to Hezekiah, "Yes you can, young man, but God has shown mercy on you. In thankfulness you must also show mercy on your neighbors. You should sell them for two lepta each."

"You're right Jesus, that's a great idea! Everybody will have a lamb! Oh, thank you, God."

18

Turning the Tables

Thursday, 10 April AD 27, 9:00 am

John followed Jesus through the Huldah gates and up the stairway leading to the Court of the Foreigners. The going was slow, as all the entrances to the temple grounds were packed with people coming and going. But Jesus wanted to visit the temple today. They emerged into the courtyard among the frenzy of buyers looking for unblemished lambs and oxen and doves. In spite of the inflated prices of Passover season, people were still buying. Even the moneychangers were taking an extra cut of profit today. Jesus stood and looked at the merchants.

Then John was shocked at what Jesus did: He took the cords around his tunic and made them into a whip. With the whip, Jesus drove out the sheep and the cattle, and overturned the tables of the moneychangers, scattering their coins across the courtyard. And to those selling doves, he said, "Take these things away! Stop making my Father's house into a place of business!"

The police at the temple doors froze in confusion, unable to move. No one had done such a thing before. Then the captain of the guard, followed by two of his lieutenants, came running from the temple, drawing his sword as he ran. He came up to Jesus and demanded, "What sign do you show us as your authority for doing these things?"

Jesus faced the naked steel and said: "Destroy this temple, and in three days I will raise it again."

One of the lieutenants said, "It took forty-six years to build this temple, and you are going to raise it up in three days?" [44]

"You know not what you are saying, nor to whom you are speaking," said Jesus, and he turned to leave. John was angered by the threat to Jesus, and followed him closely. But the three policemen stayed put.

When they reached the stairway, John noticed two men following them. Jesus turned and said to them, "What do you seek?"

One of them said, "Great teacher, where are you staying?"

Jesus broke out into a smile. "Come and see," he said.

Going down the stairs, Jesus asked them, "Have you joined a group for the Passover feast yet?"

"No, teacher," they said.

"Good. Come and join our group, for there are only eight of us, plus an infant. We must have ten people to properly observe the Passover. I am Jesus of Nazareth, and this is John son of Zebedee. Tell us your names."

The taller man said, "I am Simon of Hebron in Judea. I was a member of the Zealot party that's forming to cast out the Roman overlords. I stopped going to Zealot meetings when they became infested with members of the Sicarii party, who carry hidden daggers to kill Roman sympathizers. I can't believe that sticking a dagger into a Roman is going to bring the Messiah to Israel any sooner, and we are lost without the Messiah."

The shorter man said, "I am Judas of Kerioth in Judea. Simon took me to one of the Zealot meetings. But like Simon, I look first for the Messiah, who will set all things straight."

19

Passover Feast

Friday, 11 April AD 27, 6:00 am

It was the morning before Passover. Hezekiah was on his way with John to sacrifice the Passover lamb. Simon and Judas came with them to be their bodyguards in the crush of people at the temple.

Hezekiah had bought the forty lambs from Joseph, and then sold thirty-nine of them to families in the City of David, the slum district of Jerusalem. He made a profit of one lepton each. In turn, shares in each of the lambs were sold to yet others, so that each lamb was shared among multiple families. The lamb that Hezekiah was leading was going to be shared among six families on his alley. Not one Jewish family in the City of David would go without a Passover feast this year.

There were no merchants in the foreigners' courtyard, for buying and selling were forbidden on this day. Inside the temple a large chorus of Levites was singing psalms while the sacrifices were being conducted. There were twelve lines of men leading lambs, waiting their turn to be served by twelve sets of priests at the railing in front of the altar.

Each man would slay his lamb, and cut a piece of fat that he handed to a priest. A second priest would catch some of the blood in a dish. That priest would hand the dish to a third priest who would carry it to the altar, and a fourth priest would pour the blood on the side of the base of the altar, while a fifth priest was carrying a dish back to the priest gathering sacrificial blood. The owner of the slaughtered lamb would then hoist it over his shoulders and leave the temple.

There was no time today for the priests to extort their bribes from the sacrificers.

Hezekiah reached the front of the line, and said to the priest, "I present this lamb as a sacrifice in remembrance of the Passover in Egypt." John helped him wield the knife to kill the lamb. Hezekiah was visibly shaken; he had never killed anything before.

"Your sacrifice is accepted for the glory of God," said the priest. The dead lamb was too heavy for Hezekiah, so John heaved it up onto his shoulders, and walked with their group out of the temple. Descending the steps outside he almost stumbled and fell, but Simon caught him.

"Here, let me help," said Simon, who took the dead lamb from John and carried it.

"John, how long have you been a disciple of Jesus?" asked Simon.

"Not long," John said, "less than a month."

Judas said, "Simon and I were amazed at the power that this man Jesus can use. He marched right into the Court of the Foreigners and did whatever he wanted to do, and nobody could stop him. Could he be the Messiah?"

"That has not been revealed, Judas," said John.

"Well, that's the kind of power that'll be needed if we're ever going to shake off the rule of Rome and have our own king again in Israel," said Judas.

Abigail and two other women were roasting the Passover lamb over an open pit fire behind her house. She left the women to their tasks and called to her children.

"Come, children!" she called. "We must search the house for leaven! Rebekah, Rachel, Come! David! Dan! Come help! Look in every corner of the house to see if you can find any of the leaven that we use to make our bread rise."

"Oh, Mom," said Dan, "why do we have to do this?"

David said to him, "Don't you know, Dan? When our fathers were set free from Egypt they didn't have enough time to wait for the bread to rise. So on Passover we burn all the leaven, and eat crackers instead of bread."

"The one who finds leaven will get a prize," said Abigail.

That did the trick. They searched every nook and cranny of their tiny home, and were rewarded when they found the bits of leaven that Abigail had strategically hidden.

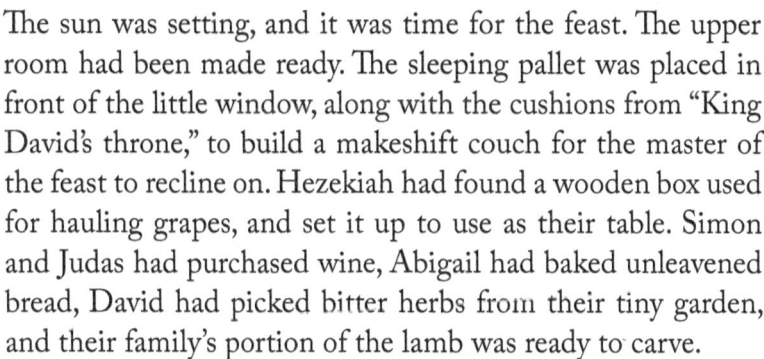

The sun was setting, and it was time for the feast. The upper room had been made ready. The sleeping pallet was placed in front of the little window, along with the cushions from "King David's throne," to build a makeshift couch for the master of the feast to recline on. Hezekiah had found a wooden box used for hauling grapes, and set it up to use as their table. Simon and Judas had purchased wine, Abigail had baked unleavened bread, David had picked bitter herbs from their tiny garden, and their family's portion of the lamb was ready to carve.

John was at the bottom of the stairs, with a towel and a bowl of water. As each person came to the stairs, John removed their sandals and washed their feet. When John took his own seat, there were eleven of them: Jesus, John, Simon, Judas, Abigail, Hezekiah, David, Dan, Rebekah, Rachel, and baby Deborah. Hezekiah reclined at the head of the table.

Jesus poured wine into a cup, and held it up, saying the first blessing: "Blessed are you, Lord God, King of the Universe, who brings forth the fruit of the vine!" And each person drank some wine from their own cup.

Then Abigail passed around a plate with bitter herbs, and David remembered that was his cue to ask the first question. He asked, "Why do we eat bitter herbs on this night?"

Hezekiah said, "We eat bitter herbs on this night to remind us that life was bitter when our fathers were slaves in Egypt."

The evening was festive rather than solemn, and everyone enjoyed the meal, including the unleavened crackers and the lamb meat. Meat was rarely seen at Abigail's house.

At the close of the meal Jesus said the final blessing over the fourth cup of wine, and passed the cup around so that all could share in the same blessing.

Hezekiah said, "This has been the best night ever!"

And John had just celebrated his fourteenth Passover.

20

NICODEMUS AT NIGHT

SATURDAY, 12 APRIL AD 27, 8:00 AM

John and Jesus were at the synagogue early again, although not as early as last week. Simon and Judas had said they would be along shortly. Hezekiah said he would bring his brother David with him again, which would relieve his mother, having one less child to keep track of.

A young man about John's age approached John on the steps of the synagogue. "Hello," he said, "Are you the disciple of Jesus of Nazareth?"

"Yes I am," John said. "I am John, son of Zebedee."

"I am Elnathan of Emmaus, and I'm a disciple of Nicodemus, the great teacher and member of the Supreme Council of Israel. Nicodemus would like to meet with your teacher here tonight, at four hours after sundown."

"Just a minute," John said. He went to find Jesus, who was inside talking with Rabbi Yanai about the poor people of the City of David.

John waited silently at Jesus' side until they finished talking. Then Jesus turned to John and said, "Tell Elnathan I will see his master at the hour he has requested."

John opened his mouth. Then he closed his mouth. Then he went back to Elnathan and told him the meeting had been arranged.

John enjoyed the synagogue meeting, especially because all of Jesus' disciples from Galilee showed up: Simon Peter with his wife Concordia, John's big brother James, Andrew, Philip, and Nathanael with his cousin Matthias. To his surprise, the Alpheus family came also: small James, Joses, and Thaddeus. Along with Simon the Zealot and Judas of Kerioth, they introduced themselves to one another, trying to sort out all the names. Hezekiah and David were hanging around the edge with John and Thaddeus.

Nathanael said, "Okay we've got two guys named James here; we're going to have to call you Big James and Little James! Not to mention the James that's not here, Jesus' brother. So which one of us is the first?"

"Thaddeus is the first," said John. "He is the first one who recognized Jesus."

Jesus said, "Whether you're the first or the last, if you're with me, we will be leaving for the wilds of Judea in the morning. But you sons of Malchiel must stay here under subjection to your mother Abigail. We're going to a place where there is much water, and Judeans will be coming out to hear the *Son of Adam*."

The moon was full and bright, and John was waiting with Jesus in the moon shadow on the southern steps leading up to the Synagogue of David. Nicodemus was late.

John asked Jesus, "Isn't Nicodemus one of the leading Pharisees?"

"Yes he is, John," Jesus said, "but he's one of the better ones. He has a true heart for the orphans and the widows. He's also a member of the great council of the Jews, but he can do little there among so many with hardened hearts."

Nicodemus appeared on the street followed by Elnathan, and climbed up the steps. He extended his right hand and clasped Jesus' hand, saying "Jesus of Galilee, I'm pleased to meet you. I have heard of great things you've been doing in the City of David. Many people know I have land holdings in Galilee. My business associate Maimon administers my farmlands near Cana, and he tells me he has a strange surplus of wine after your visit there. And tongues are wagging after your recent escapade in the Court of the Foreigners."

Then his voice dropped, and in a serious tone he said, "Great teacher, we know you have come from God to teach us, for no one can do these signs you do unless God is with him."

Jesus said, "In truth I tell you, unless one is born again from above, he cannot see the kingdom of God."

Nicodemus said, "How can a man be born when he is old? He can't enter a second time into his mother's womb and be born, can he?"

Jesus said, "In truth I tell you, unless one is born of water and the Spirit he cannot enter the kingdom of God. That which is born of the flesh is flesh, and that which is born of the Spirit is spirit. Don't be amazed that I said you must be born again from above. The wind blows where it will, and you hear it, but don't know from where it comes or where it is going. So it is with everyone who is born of the Spirit."

Nicodemus said, "How can these things be?"

Jesus said, "You are the teacher of Israel and you don't understand these things? In truth I tell you, we speak of what we know and testify of what we have seen, but you don't accept our testimony. If I told you earthly things and you don't believe, how will you believe if I tell you heavenly things?

"No one has ascended into heaven but he who descended from heaven, the *Son of Adam*. As Moses lifted up the serpent in the wilderness, even so must the *Son of Adam* be lifted up, so that whoever believes in him will have eternal life."[45]

"These are weighty matters," Nicodemus said, "and I know you can say only what you have been given by God to say. But I cannot protect you forever from the Supreme Council."

Jesus said, "I have a cup to drink, and no man can take away that cup."

Jesus and John watched in silence as Nicodemus and Elnathan disappeared up the street.

John had much to think about. But he resolved to ask Jesus why he always switched from the Aramaic language into Hebrew each time he used the phrase *Son of Adam*, for *Adam* in Hebrew was usually translated "man" or "humanity" in Aramaic or in Greek.

21

ON THE ROAD AGAIN

SUNDAY, 13 APRIL AD 27, 10:00 AM

Jesus was well in front of the expedition, while Peter was bringing up the rear. John was walking with Thaddeus, and asked him, "Tad, have you heard any news about the Baptist?"

Thaddeus said, "Oh, yes! He moved! You haven't heard? My dad found out that the Sadducees he insulted made the owner of the Bethabara Ferry kick him out. He moved to Salim in Samaria, where there's a spring with a lot of water. Maybe he'll be safer there, in Roman territory instead of near the territory of Herod Antipas."

"Are people finding him there?"

"Yes, but not as many," Thaddeus said. "People are finding out that Jesus is the 'greater one' that the Baptist was talking about, and they've been looking for Jesus. It prob'ly won't be long before they're looking for him out here."

"Hey, I just remembered a question I wanna ask Jesus. I'll be back." John ran ahead to catch up with Jesus, and said, "Teacher, I have a question."

"Yes, John?"

"I was wondering, why do you call yourself the 'Son of Man?'"

"Tell me, John, if you take off your sandals and walk over stones, does it hurt your feet?"

"Yes."

"When I walk over stones without my sandals, my feet hurt too. I am a man like you."

"Oh. But, why do you say it in Hebrew, *'ben Adam'*?"

"Ah, that is a two part parable, and to you it's granted to know the meaning. First, I *am* a descendant of the first man Adam, so he is my father. But Adam had no father except the Father in heaven. I too have the Father in heaven for my father, and I have been sent to set aright the wrong that Adam and his descendants have done."

"Wow. That's a heavy burden. I was thinking of the burden Hezekiah will be taking when he becomes head of his family, but it's nothing compared to yours."

"You have judged correctly, John."

"But Teacher, you said there were two parts."

"Yes. I could identify myself in Aramaic, *bar enash*, a Son of Man. But one day I will say that, and it will get me killed."

"What! How is that?" John was disturbed.

"The prophet Daniel writes that one like a *bar enash* will come with the clouds of heaven." [46]

"This is confusing to me, not plain at all." John said.

"It will become more plain to you if you will read more scripture," said Jesus.

22

Baptizing in Judea

Monday, 14 April AD 27, 7:00 am

John and Andrew were standing at the top of a cliff, looking over the great expanse of the Dead Sea below them. Andrew asked, "Where are we, anyway, John?"

"This place is called Ein Feshkha, the cliff-top spring," John said. "Those abandoned houses we're camped at were built by the Essenes, but they left long ago. And Herod the Great built a house near here too, but it's empty now. The shepherds that helped bring our Passover lambs told us about this place. Only shepherds come here anymore, to water their sheep."

"Isn't there an Essene town near here somewhere?"

"Yes, Qumran. It's only a couple miles away."

Andrew said, "Oh! I hear my brother calling! Let's go back."

Jesus was gathering the disciples together for a teaching. They collected next to an ancient walled water pool, which was fed by the nearby spring. He sat on a wall and asked the gathering, "What do you know about the messenger of God? What is his name? What is he called?"

"He's called the Messiah, of whom the prophet Daniel wrote," said Judas of Kerioth.[47]

"Or Elijah, of whom the prophet Malachi wrote," said Simon of Hebron.[48]

"Then there's the one like Moses, of whom God spoke," said James of Zebedee.[49]

"And the angel Gabriel, who spoke to your mother," said Concordia. [50]

"Or the blind and deaf one, of whom the prophet Isaiah wrote," said Nathanael.[51]

"Very good," said Jesus. "I have another for you to consider of whom Isaiah wrote, saying,

> Surely it was our sufferings he bore,
> and our sorrows he carried,
> yet we considered him stricken,
> struck down by God, and afflicted.
> But he was pierced for our transgressions;
> he was crushed for our iniquities;
> the punishment which made us whole was upon him,
> and by his bruises we are healed.
> All of us like sheep have gone astray,
> each of us has turned to his own way;
> and the Lord has laid on him the iniquity of us all.[52]

"The interpretation of this is, before we can deal with the misdeeds of the Romans, we must deal with our own misdeeds. Before we can cast doubt on the hearts of the Samaritans, we must search our own hearts. Before we can question the Greeks, we must question ourselves. And before there is salvation, there must be repentance. This is the good news I bring, for salvation from sin is near.

"The kingdom of God is at hand, and the time is short. Who will sound the alarm? Who will wake up Judea? Who will arouse Galilee? The Baptist has begun the task, who will join in?"

John shifted his feet uncomfortably. The others also were uncomfortable.

Jesus continued, "So today we will start practicing. Most of you have heard John the Baptist preach, and most of you have taken the baptism of John. Today one of you will preach as you have heard him preach, and as you have heard me. Then you will baptize those who are ready to repent. Who will be the first to preach?"

More feet shuffling.

"Ah yes, so I thought. So I will choose. Concordia, you will be the first to preach."

Concordia exclaimed, "Oh, no, teacher, I cannot!"

"Do not be afraid, Concordia. Just look out over these men, and pretend they are a group of women gathered in your kitchen. Speak the words you have already heard."

Concordia stood up, and began uncertainly, but as she went on, her voice became more powerful and she waded into her sermon with gusto.

When she finished, Simon the Zealot, Judas of Kerioth, and Matthias nephew of Tholmai were baptized, with Simon Peter and Andrew conducting the baptism in the rock-lined pool.[53]

The days passed by at Ein Feshkha, with each disciple learning how to preach. When they had done so, Jesus released them to go and tend to their businesses, telling them to be ready to spread the good news any time they had a chance. Some of them, such as Joses, left as soon as they were released, while others, such as John, remained with Jesus.

A trickle of people began to appear to hear Jesus preach, and before long the trickle had become a flood. Some of the newly baptized stayed to learn how to preach the good news, and waited to be released before leaving. One of them, called Thomas the Twin, took the training and was released, but he would not depart, saying, "I will not leave my Lord, in whom there is life." Another who remained was a friend of Simon the Zealot: Joseph of Hebron, son of Sabbas.[54]

News came from Salim, where John the Baptist had learned that the disciples with Jesus were baptizing more people than the Baptist. He had begun preaching, "I am not the Messiah, but I have been sent ahead of him. He who has the bride is the bride-groom, but the friend of the bride-groom, who stands and hears him, rejoices greatly when he hears the bride-groom's voice. Therefore this joy of mine has been made complete. He must increase, but I must decrease."[55]

23

BAD NEWS

Thursday, 29 May AD 27, 2:00 pm

"Look! It's Daniel!" John was standing on the cliff with Thaddeus, and had just spotted two disciples of John the Baptist coming up the trail from the Dead Sea. "Hey, Daniel!"

Daniel waved back, but did not seem joyous. When he arrived at the cliff top, John could see that his face was somber. He asked, "What's wrong, Daniel?"

"Bad news, John," Daniel said. "The prophet has been thrown into Herod Antipas' prison."

"Oh, no! What happened? Did he travel into Herod's territory?"

"No, not at all," Daniel said. "The Jewish party of the Herodians talked Governor Pilate into sending a squad of Roman soldiers to arrest him at Salim. They gave him to Herod's men, who took him to Fort Machaerus on the other side of the Dead Sea. You can see the fort from here. It's a big palace."

John said, "I wonder if those two rich Sadducees had something to do with it?"

"Yes, they're the ones who put the Herodians up to it," Daniel said. "The jail keeper at Machaerus lets us go in to see the prophet and take him food and stuff. The prophet asked us to greet Jesus and tell him what happened, and bring back news about what Jesus was doing. Oh, and he sent something for you, too."

"Oh, what is it?" asked John.

"He sent the Isaiah *pesher* scroll you were reading. He said he doesn't know how long Herod is going to keep him alive, and he wanted you to have it."

"Has he been sentenced to death?"

"No. Herod's been visiting the prophet at his jail cell and listening to him. I think he's afraid of the prophet, or superstitious about killing him." [56]

"Wow, this is not good. But out here we've been doing well so far. We're preaching and baptizing a lot of people and listening to Jesus teach. We're just a day's walk from Jerusalem, so all of Judea's been coming to hear him, and he's healed many of their sicknesses."

John brought the two disciples of the Baptist to Jesus so they could deliver their message. After hearing, Jesus asked Peter to call all his disciples together.

When they had assembled, Jesus said, "The time of the Baptist is coming to its close, and the time of revelation is before us. Prepare to travel, for tomorrow we go to Jerusalem, and the next day we will celebrate the Festival of Weeks,[57] remembering how God gave us his word by the hand of Moses. And then we will go to Galilee."[58]

24

WOMAN AT THE WELL

MONDAY, 2 JUNE AD 27, 12:00 NOON

Jesus was tired, and sat down on a rock near a well. He and his disciples had reached the ancient well of patriarch Jacob, near the Samaritan town of Sychar. It had been a busy few days.

They had left Ein Feshkha with some 20 disciples, and celebrated the Festival of Weeks in Jerusalem. Most of the new disciples from Judea returned to their homes the following day. The rest continued with Jesus through Samaria toward Galilee. Little James and his son Thaddeus stopped in Ephraim, while Nathanael and Matthias went on ahead to Cana. This left nine of them: Peter and Concordia, Andrew, Philip, Thomas, Simon the Zealot, Judas of Kerioth, and the sons of Zebedee.

Peter said, "My pack is empty. Teacher, shall we go into town to buy food?"

Jesus said, "Yes, go ahead. I will wait here with John."

The June sun was bearing down on Jesus and John, but the disciples had taken the drinking water with them into town. John could see water at the bottom of the well, but there was no way to reach it.

A Samaritan woman came from town to draw water, and Jesus said, "Give me a drink."

The woman was surprised, for Jews normally would have no dealings with Samaritans if they could avoid it. She said, "You're evidently a Jew, and I'm a Samaritan and a woman. Why would you be asking me for a drink?"

Jesus said, "Ah, if only you knew the gift God has for you and to whom you are speaking. Then *you* would ask of *me*, and *I* would give *you* a drink of *living* water."

"But sir," she said, "You don't have a rope or a bucket, and this well is deep. Where would you get this 'living water?'"

Jesus said, "Anyone who drinks the water here will soon be thirsty again. But if you drink the water I give, you will never be thirsty. The water I give will become in you a fountain springing up to eternal life."

"Sir, give me some of this water, so I won't get thirsty and have to come all this way from town to draw from a well."

"Go and get your husband," said Jesus, "so I may talk to both of you."

"I have no husband," she said.

"Yes, you are correct, you don't have a husband. For you have had five husbands, and you aren't even married to the man you're living with now. You have spoken truthfully."

"Sir, I see you must be a prophet. So can you tell me: although my ancestors have worshipped here at Mount Gerizim for many generations, why is it you Jews insist Jerusalem is the only place to worship?"

"Believe me, woman, the time is coming when you will worship the Father neither here nor in Jerusalem. You worship what you don't know. We worship what we know, for salvation comes through the Jews.

"But the time is coming," Jesus continued, "and is now upon us, when true worshippers will worship the Father in spirit and in truth. The Father is calling such worshippers. God is Spirit, so those who worship him must worship in spirit and in truth."

The woman said, "I know Messiah is coming—the one called Christ in the Greek. When he comes, he will straighten this all out and explain it to us."

"I am the Messiah," Jesus said.

Just then his disciples returned from town. They were surprised that Jesus was talking to a Samaritan woman, but they didn't have the nerve to ask him about it. The woman left her water jar beside the well, and ran into town.

The disciples broke out the food, and Concordia said, "Here, Teacher, eat something."

"I have food to eat that you know nothing about," said Jesus.

Andrew asked John, "Did someone bring him food while we were gone?"

But Jesus said, "My food is to do the will of the one who sent me and to carry out his work. Raise your eyes, and look on these fields ready for harvest! Whoever harvests these fields receives his wages and gathers fruit for eternal life. This way, the one who plants and the one who harvests can rejoice together. I am sending you to harvest where you didn't plant, so you may join with those who rejoice."

Meanwhile, the woman had gone into town telling everyone, "Come see a man who told me everything I ever did! Isn't this the Messiah? Come and see!"

Many Samaritans believed what the woman was saying. They sent a delegation to Jesus asking him to stay with them. Jesus and his disciples stayed with the Samaritans in Sychar for two nights, and many more listened to Jesus and came to believe in him.

The Samaritans who believed in Jesus told the woman, "We heard what you said about this man. Now we've heard him for ourselves, and we know he most surely is Savior of the world." [59]

One of the them, the mother of a wealthy merchant, came and laid a bag of coins at Jesus' feet. She said, "Lord, this is to sustain you and your disciples as you gather your harvest."

Jesus said, "Simon of Hebron, carry this gift for us."

Simon said, "Oh, Lord, I took an oath when I was among the Zealots not to defile myself by any money with a Roman image or inscription, until the end of this year."

"Very well, Simon, you must honor your oath. Judas of Kerioth, you will carry the purse for us."

25

Back in Galilee

SATURDAY, 7 JUNE AD 27, 9:00 AM

John and the other disciples followed Jesus into the synagogue of Nain. When they had arrived at the village the Galileans of Nain gave Jesus a big welcome. They had heard of all the things he did at the festival in Jerusalem, for they had been at the festival themselves. They had begged him to stay and heal and teach, and he stayed two nights with his disciples.

When it came time for the reading of the Haftarah, the leader of the synagogue handed a scroll to Jesus. Jesus stood up, opened the scroll and said, "The prophet Isaiah has written,

> There will be no more gloom for those who were in distress.
> In the past he humbled this land of Zebulon and Naphtali,
> But in the future he will honor Galilee of the Foreigners.
> By the way of the sea, along the banks of the Jordan,
> The people who walk in darkness will see a great light;

Those who live in the shadow of death will have light shine upon them." [60]

Jesus looked up and said, "In your ears and before your eyes, this prophecy has been fulfilled this very day." Then he read again from the scroll, saying, "And again Isaiah writes,

> A child will be born to us, a son will be given us; and the government will rest on his shoulders; and his name will be called
> Wonderful Counselor, Mighty God, Eternal Father, Prince of Peace.
> There will be no end to the increase of his government or of his peace,
> or of his reign on the throne of David and over his kingdom,
> to establish it and to uphold it with justice and righteousness, from that time on and forevermore.
> The zeal of the Lord of Heaven's Armies will accomplish this."[61]

Jesus returned the scroll, sat down and said, "Again, in your ears and before your eyes, this prophecy has begun its fulfillment in this very generation.

"So tell me, by whose zeal will this be accomplished? By the zeal of the party of the Pharisees? I tell you, No. By the zeal of the party of the Zealots? Certainly not. It says, 'by the zeal of the Lord of Heaven's Armies.'

"Don't wait for someone else to arrive. The time is now! The kingdom of God is upon you! Believe the good news! Repent! Forgive, so you may be forgiven! Begin this very day to bear forth fruits of repentance." [62]

The people were amazed at the teaching Jesus brought. Outside the synagogue they gathered around him, and some asked to be healed of their sickness.

When he was finally alone with his disciples, he said, "Friends, the time of the kingdom is coming upon us. Go ahead of me into Capernaum, and arrange lodging for Simon and Judas and Thomas. Other disciples will be coming, so prepare yourselves for a time of gathering. Go! Except for John son of Zebedee. He will follow in a few days."

26

LEAVING HOME

Tuesday, 10 June AD 27, 4:00 pm

"Son, welcome home! To tell the truth, I've been expecting you. Hello John, welcome!"

Jesus embraced his mother. "Yes, mother, you know I have unfinished business here."

"Yes," she answered. "You know, knocking about in this empty house has got me thinking about Perpetua. She's around my age, and she's been knocking about in that big house of hers with only Mina for company. I think I'd like to pay her another visit. Besides, I suspect she will soon need help taking care of lots of visitors."

"Mother, you are always more perceptive than you let on. Yes, we're going to Perpetua's house. But are you ready for an extended stay?"

"Yes, I was thinking the same thing. I've even been doing some packing."

"Mother, you're a marvel. I'm going to go down the road and borrow some donkeys from our neighbor to carry your stuff, and mine too. I've been missing my scrolls."

"Ah, so I thought," said Mary. "You're packing out of here also. I considered packing your stuff but then I remembered how it used to bother you when I organized your room."

Jesus said, "I'll leave you John to talk to for now. We'll leave on the morning after Sabbath."

Jesus left John at the door, and Mary said, "Come on in! It's good to see you."

John said, "Are you alone here? I thought Jesus' brother James lived here."

Mary said, "James and Joseph have gone to Jerusalem. They're going to try to settle the Jerusalem Pharisees down a bit; they've been raising a fuss."

"Oh, what happened? How'd James and Joseph get involved?"

"It's all about what happened at Passover with the lack of lambs for the City of David. The Pharisees preach about taking care of orphans and widows; it's one of the foundation stones of their teachings. So when help had to come all the way from Galilee to solve their own problem, they lost honor. It's a disgrace for them."

"So James and Joseph went because they brought the lambs?"

Mary said, "Well, not really. James has helped several villages to organize how they care for widows and orphans, so he has experience with that. He should be able to help them with how the city of David got overlooked so badly. But to tell the truth, I think the Pharisees are trying to place all the blame on Jesus, even though it was Joseph who had the dream."

John exclaimed, "Blame it on Jesus? What did he do?"

"It seems word got out that he had prophesied that God would provide a lamb. Some of the Pharisees think it was all a prearranged plot to make them look bad. They'll do anything to make it look like it wasn't their own fault, instead of just confessing their sin."

"Are Simon and Jude at home? I thought I might visit with their kids a bit."

"No, they're staying in Sepphoris working on a big construction project. The work pays very well, and they'll be back in time for harvest. But their wives and kids are at home."

27

Nazareth Rejection

SATURDAY, 14 JUNE AD 27, 8:00 AM

"John, I want to thank you for all the help you've been in packing up. Did you have fun visiting Simon and Jude's kids?"

"You're welcome, Mary. Yeah, I had a good visit yesterday. But I found out that some of the men in the village have been grumbling about Jesus leaving town."

"Oh? What have they been saying?"

"They heard about the healings Jesus did in Capernaum, and were thinking that he was coming to do the same here. I guess they've been expecting Jesus to move back to Nazareth and be the resident town doctor."

Mary said, "Then they must be blind. There are great things about to take place that are a lot bigger than a country doctor with a sure-fire cure for the sniffles. They have no concept of who Jesus really is."

"You're right, mother Mary. That's the problem for sure."

"I hope things turn out all right. I'm going to do some more arranging here, so I'll see you and Jesus when you get back from synagogue."

Jesus stood up to read, and the scroll of the prophet Isaiah was handed to him. He unrolled the scroll and read aloud:

> The Spirit of the Lord is upon me,
> Because he has anointed me to preach good news to the poor.
> He has sent me to proclaim release to the captives,
> And recovery of sight to the blind,
> To set free those who are oppressed,
> To proclaim the favorable year of the Lord. [63]

Then he rolled up the scroll, gave it back to the attendant, and sat down. All the eyes in the synagogue were on him.

And Jesus said, "Today this scripture has been fulfilled in your hearing."

Everyone wondered at these words of grace. But some were offended, saying, "Isn't this just the son of Joseph?"

Another one said, "This is the skinny little kid who grew up right here in town."

Jesus said, "No doubt you will quote this proverb to me, 'Doctor, heal yourself! Do the same things in your hometown that you did in Capernaum.' Truly I tell you, no prophet is accepted in his hometown."

"But I tell you the truth," he continued, "There were many widows in Israel in the days of Elijah, when the rain didn't fall for three and a half years, and a great famine came over the land; and yet Elijah was sent to none of them, but only to a widow in the foreign land of Sidon.

"And there were many lepers in Israel in the time of Elisha the prophet, and none of them was healed, but only Naaman from the foreign land of Syria."

The men in the synagogue were filled with anger as they heard these words, and they got up and drove him out of the synagogue, intending to throw him down the hillside.

But Jesus waved them aside, and passed through their midst untouched.⁶⁴

John was being ignored by the crowd while this was happening. A rising fury grew up inside him as he struggled to get near Jesus. When the crowd parted, John hurried to his side as he strode down the hill to the house.

Back in the house, John said, "Jesus, that was awful! Why didn't you strike them down?"

"Oh my child, what you saw was only the smallest part of what was actually happening. They had envy in their hearts for the healings in Capernaum, and the Enemy was using that to stir up their anger. He was trying to tempt me to strike out at my neighbors in anger. But that is not my mission, and I passed the test. The Enemy captured no hearts today"

"Oh, Wow." John was dumbfounded. "Still, they didn't have to do all that."

"Here, John, take this and put it in your pack. It's the scroll of the prophet Daniel. It will answer some of your questions, but you will have more questions after you have read it than before."

"Why is that, teacher?"

"Daniel writes of what will happen in the time to come. But the Father has not revealed when these things will take place. Many read Daniel and wonder what it means. But after the things in this scroll take place, men will look in it and find that it happened just as he had written.

"And some day you too, John, will be overpowered by the hand of the Father, and you too will write of things that will take place. Men will interpret what you write in many ways, but after the things take place they will see that your writings were true."

"But teacher," John asked, "If the Father wants to keep things hidden, why does he have the prophets write of them?"

"When the prophet's words come to pass," said Jesus, "then no man can say, 'this happened by chance,' or 'God did not do this.'"

"I see, teacher. Thank you."

"Tomorrow, John, you and my mother will take the donkeys and go ahead of me to Capernaum. I will go to Cana, and I'll join you in Capernaum later. I must preach in Cana next week. Spend time with your family, John, and watch over my mother on your journey."

28

What's Wrong with Mom?

Monday, 16 June AD 27, 3:00 pm

John and Mary had stopped at a small inn near the ruins of the ancient city of Madon, before continuing the next day. It was a relief to knock on Perpetua's door, for Mary was weary.

Mina opened the door, and exclaimed, "Mary! John! Good to see you! Perpetua! Mary is here!"

Perpetua and Concordia came and greeted them. "You look tired, Mary," said Perpetua. "But I'm so glad you took me up on my invitation. Mina has prepared a room for you."

"Yes, Perpetua, I'm not a youngster like John anymore. But I'll be fine when I get some rest."

"The men are on the lake, but they'll be back before nightfall. Come sit, have a cup of tea."

John was at the shore watching for Peter's boat, and waved when he saw it. Big James left the others securing the boat, gave John a big bear hug, and walked up to the house with him.

"Hey, bro, it's good to see you," he said, "Dad's been getting impatient; he says we're gonna need your help. And mom is all ticked off."

"What's wrong with Mom?"

"Well, like Dad, she was expecting you home a lot sooner. But she doesn't like it that you got assigned to be Jesus' lowest disciple. She says it's an insult, especially because there are newer disciples than you and younger ones, too. She says it's an insult to our family honor."

John said, "Actually, I kind of like what I'm doing. I get to spend one-on-one time with Jesus, and I've been getting teachings that some of the others aren't getting."

"Yea, that's what I figured," said James. "But Mom doesn't see it that way."

John asked, "So what's up with Dad? Am I in trouble again?"

"No, not really," James said. "It's just that he's finally got his big long-line dragnet again, and he's impatient to try it out. We haven't been catching much at all with the throw nets. We're going to be using all three boats, ours and Peter's and Philip's, and we need all hands on deck."

The rest of the men caught up with them: Peter, Andrew, Philip, and Simon the Zealot.

"Hey Simon," said John, "I didn't know you were a fisherman!"

"I'm not," Simon said. "Peter's been trying to teach me how to handle a boat, but I'm not very good at it. They put me on the tiller today because I kept getting my oar tangled with everyone else's. I'm a certified landlubber."

John laughed at him. "You'll catch on, Simon. This is going to be fun, using the big net."

Perpetua passed them at the door, saying, "I'm going over to the Lord Mayor's house. His little boy is very sick, and I'm going to see if I can help my friend Portia, his wife."

29

MAYOR ON A HORSE

TUESDAY, 17 JUNE AD 27, 8:00 AM

John was looking out over the Sea of Galilee from Perpetua's porch, watching seagulls swarming around someone's fishing boat far out on the lake. That was a sure sign fish had been caught, and the men were sorting their catch, throwing out anything unusable.

Concordia and Perpetua had risen earlier and gone up the Roman road leading to Lord Mayor Jaroel's house. They had gone to check on his little son and see what they could do to help.

Suddenly John heard the clatter of horse's hooves coming down the stone-paved road. It was the Lord Mayor astride a horse, not dressed in his usual finery but wearing simple riding clothes. He had a grim face as he urged his horse on. He turned south along the lakeside road and disappeared out of sight at a thundering gallop. A minute later, Concordia came down the road. John asked, "Concordia, what's happening?"

"Jaroel's little boy is burning with fever, and getting weaker," said Concordia. "We're afraid he's dying. I told Jaroel about the people Jesus healed when he was in Capernaum, and what you told me, that Jesus is in Cana now. Right away, Jaroel called for his horse and rode off."

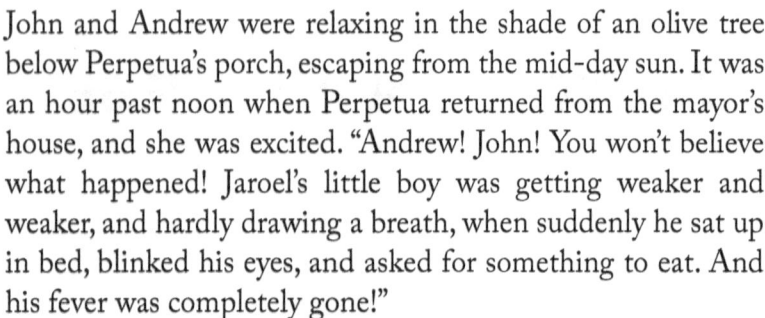

John and Andrew were relaxing in the shade of an olive tree below Perpetua's porch, escaping from the mid-day sun. It was an hour past noon when Perpetua returned from the mayor's house, and she was excited. "Andrew! John! You won't believe what happened! Jaroel's little boy was getting weaker and weaker, and hardly drawing a breath, when suddenly he sat up in bed, blinked his eyes, and asked for something to eat. And his fever was completely gone!"

"Oh, wow," said John. "That's wonderful."

"Two of the mayor's servants left right away to Cana to tell Jaroel that his son lives," said Perpetua. "I left my friend Paula to stay at Portia's side, for she is exhausted. Paula is the wife of Matthew, Herod's tax collector. And I'm not feeling well myself. I'm going to bed for a bit."

Just as dusk was closing in, Jaroel rode up to Perpetua's gate, and shouted, "Hello the house!"

Simon Peter went out the door, followed by Andrew and John. Peter said, "Yes, lord?"

"Simon, tell your wife that my son lives! Today at one hour after noontime, Jesus of Nazareth said to me 'Your son lives,' and my servants tell me he was healed at that very hour." [65]

"We are very grateful, lord," Peter said, "God is good."

"Yes he is, and I will be showing my gratitude to you and your wife for leading me to Jesus."

30

CATCHING FISH

Thursday, 26 June AD 27, 1:00 am

Tonight was the big night. They had been on three boat runs this week in daylight to practice deploying the big net. The net fabric was specially designed to be invisible in the water at night, but it would scare the fish away in daylight.

The construction of the net itself was Zebedee's own invention, with weights at the bottom and floats at the top. It would be let out at each end by two big boats that would pull it into a circle and draw it closed around a school of fish. A third, smaller boat would be used to hold the mid-point of the net in place while the large boats were drawing it around the fish. When the net was full of fish, cords were used to close it at the bottom, and then the net with the fish would be hauled into one of the large boats.

It was important to maintain silence so as not to scare the fish. Simon the Zealot had almost mastered the art of propelling the boat with a silent pull on the oars. Judas of Kerioth was working with Philip in his smaller boat, and he was getting better at it also. To keep silence, Zebedee would use hand signals to direct the other boats as they made their scripted maneuvers.

But the biggest factor was finding the big schools of fish in the first place. Zebedee was the recognized master at that. It was said on the lake that if Big Thunder couldn't find any fish, there was no point in anyone else even leaving shore.

Father Zebedee was at the tiller of his boat while on its oars were his two sons, James and John, and his two long-time servants. Peter and Andrew's father Jonah no longer fished himself. Older son Peter was at the tiller of Jonah's boat, while Andrew and Simon the Zealot were at the oars along with the two hired Bashan brothers. Philip was at the oars of his own boat with Judas, who was assigned to hold the center point of the top of the net when it was deployed.

There was no moon tonight, but the sky was clear and starlight sparkled on the water. They had been rowing slowly southward, searching for fish. Finally Zebedee signaled that he had sensed a school of fish, and Jonah's boat began pulling the net out of Zebedee's boat, with the bottom weights on the net pulling it down to form an underwater wall. Judas grabbed the top center of the net and Philip held his boat's position while the crews of the two large boats began to close the circle around the fish.

Then there was a flash, and a ripple on the water. The entire school of fish had bolted out of the circling net at one time. John almost blurted out his disappointment, but then he remembered that he had to maintain silence if they were going to outwit the fish. They laboriously hauled the net back into one of the big boats, and started over.

Three more times they searched, found, and attempted to encircle a school of fish, and three more times the fish bolted and escaped. By this time the sky was beginning to lighten.

John and the Jesus Boat

Dawn was upon them, so they gave it up and returned to shore.

But there was still work to be done: the net had to be cleaned and stowed, and small tears in the net fabric had to be fixed. The net had dragged up small crabs and other shellfish, which they threw out, for Jews were prohibited from eating shellfish by their dietary laws.

By this time it was almost two hours after dawn. John looked up from his work and spotted a group of men walking toward them. When they came closer, he got excited. "James, look! It's Jesus! And Nathanael!"

Sure enough, Jesus was walking down the beach, teaching as he walked, followed closely by at least 30 people crowded around him. Nathanael and Matthias and Thomas were with him, along with some men from Cana, and some men and women from Capernaum.

Peter hailed Jesus from his boat-side, "Welcome back, Teacher!"

Jesus said, "Hello Peter! Put your boat into the water, so I may sit and teach."

Peter and Andrew complied, and all three boat crews joined in listening as Jesus taught the crowd gathered on the shore. He was teaching again about the innocent messenger from God who would be killed for the wrong-doings of others, and what that meant for his listeners.

When he had finished, he dismissed the crowd, although four stayed behind. Two of them were new disciples from Cana, and two were disciples who had come to Jesus at Ein Feshkha in Judea.

Jesus turned to Peter and said, "Simon Peter, put out your boat into the deep water and let down the nets for a catch."

Peter said, "Master, we have been on the lake fishing all night, working hard but catching nothing. But I will do as you say and let down the nets."

Zebedee wanted to try the big net again, so all three boats rowed out as Jesus and the other disciples watched from shore. They let down the net as before, but this time they closed the trap on a great quantity of fish. Peter and Andrew and the Bashan brothers tried to pull the catch into their boat, but there were so many huge fish that the net began to break.

"Zebedee," yelled Peter, "come help! There's too many fish here!" With their help, they filled both big boats with fish, and even loaded Philip's boat, until the water was almost coming over the sides of the boats. Then they struggled to row the three heavy boats back and haul them onto the shore.

There had never been such a catch as this in the memory of any of the fishermen of Galilee. All the men were struck with amazement.

Simon Peter was shaken. He went to where Jesus was standing, and threw himself at Jesus' feet. He said, "O my Lord, depart from me, for I am a sinful man!"

"Do not fear, Simon," said Jesus, "for from now on you will be catching people."[66]

And Zebedee was happy that his new net finally worked for them.

31

A Foul Spirit

Friday, 27 June AD 27, 4:00 pm

Yesterday Philip and Judas of Kerioth had rowed Philip's boat to Bethsaida, where his family had fish-drying racks that could be used for Philip's share of the catch.

The rest of the fishermen had sailed the two overloaded boats with the aid of a gentle breeze to the fish processing plant in Magdala. The plant manager had refused to buy the fish at the usual price, saying it would make an overstock that would take too long to sell. So Zebedee and Peter paid to have the fish dried and smoked and salted, to pick them up when they were ready. Zebedee was already calculating the profit he could make in Jerusalem, and planning where he might rent or buy enough donkeys to get them there.

On their return to Capernaum the fishermen had slept at Peter's house exhausted. They had been up for 40 hours, and hard at work most of that time. While they slept, James son of Alpheus and his son Judas Thaddeus arrived from Ephraim, and Joseph son of Sabbas arrived from Hebron.

Today James and John were working with Zebedee on the big net. They were repairing the rips in the net fabric caused by their big catch. Samuel and Sheva were cleaning the boat inside and out, which yesterday had been full to the brim with fish.

Peter and Andrew had been working longer than the Zebedee crew. They had finished cleaning their boat and had put out a few yards from shore, and were casting their throw nets and washing them before folding and stowing them in the boat.

John saw Jesus walking toward them and pointed him out to James. Jesus stopped near Peter's boat and called out, "Peter! Andrew! Come and follow me, and I will make you into fishers of people." They immediately beached their boat and followed Jesus.

Jesus continued down the shore to Zebedee's boat and called James and John, saying "Follow me!" They immediately left the net and the boat and followed Jesus, who was walking toward Capernaum. Zebedee and his servants stood silently, watching them go.[67]

John asked, "Master, where are we going?"

"I must teach in the Capernaum synagogue tonight," Jesus said. "Run ahead and tell the disciples lodging at Peter's house to come with us."

―――――・・●●●・・―――――

Evidently word had gotten out that Jesus would be at synagogue this night: the place was packed. Philip and Judas of Kerioth arrived just in time from Bethsaida.

John noticed that even Crazy Eddy was there in his usual corner. Eddy could be strange at times, blurting out unexpected words at inconvenient moments, and he was always nervous. He scraped out a living by cleaning boats.

The meeting began with some lusty singing of favorite psalms, and a prayer for God's blessing. After that, Jesus began to teach of the good news of the coming kingdom of God. Jesus taught with confidence and authority that amazed his listeners.

Then a loud voice startled everyone: "What business do we have with each other, Jesus of Nazareth? Have you come to destroy us? I know who you are—the Holy One of God!" The voice was coming from Crazy Eddy in the corner.

Jesus said, "You foul spirit! Be quiet! Leave this man, and never return!"[68]

With a loud cry, the man was thrown to the floor, then all the tension seemed to be released from his body. Jesus took him by the hand and lifted him to his feet, saying, "Jahath of Edrie,[69] you have been released from evil. Now rejoice, and seek the kingdom."

The people in the synagogue were astonished, and said to each other, "Who is this man? With a word of power he commands the foul spirits and they come out!"

Then Jesus left the synagogue and went to Simon Peter's house with his disciples. Jahath of Edrie followed Jesus closely, with a look of joyfulness on his face.

Mina greeted Jesus inside the door, saying, "Master, Perpetua has not been feeling well for the last few days. She has a fever, and has not been out of her bed this whole day."

"Take me to her, Mina," he said.

Mina led Jesus to Perpetua, and he stood over her saying, "Come out of her, you fever!"

Perpetua sat up and took Jesus' hand, and got out of bed. "Oh, I feel much better," she said. She followed Mina to the kitchen, and helped her prepare and serve food to Jesus and his disciples.[70]

Jahath of Edrie, no longer called "Crazy Eddie," was the guest of honor.

Concordia had noticed that the food cupboards were looking a bit bare. She approached Jesus with a question. "Teacher, Portia the mayor's wife and Paula the tax collector's wife have each given me a sack of coins in thankfulness for the healing of the mayor's little boy. What shall I do with them?

Jesus said, "Entrust the money to Judas of Kerioth. And if you need anything at all to care for my disciples, ask him and Simon the Zealot to shop for you."

"Thank you, Teacher," Concordia said, "That takes a worry off my mind."

32

Hidden Demons

SATURDAY, 28 JUNE AD 27, 6:00 PM

Today should have been a day for relaxing, but it seemed to John there was tension in the air. Almost 20 disciples were with Jesus now, most of them lodging at Peter's house. The smell of travel was almost palpable, and some of the disciples were packed ready to go. Yet there was much for Jesus to do in Capernaum, for many had come up to him at synagogue telling of family members beset by illnesses or oppressed by foul spirits.

John, Andrew, Philip, and Nathanael were sitting on a deck above the first floor of the house, talking with Jahath of Edrie as the sun was getting ready to set on the Sabbath. Philip said, "Jahath, where is the town of Edrie, anyway?"

He said, "Edrie is in the south part of Syria. In Moses' day it was the capital of Bashan."

John asked, "Oh, and is your family there?"

"Yes they are," Jahath said, "but the synagogue members drove me out of town 'cause they were afraid of me. I was hiding for a while in the old tunnels under the city where rebels hid after the invasion of Alexander the Great. But I had to beg for food. Capernaum was the first place I found that would tolerate me."

Andrew asked, "So what are you going to do now, go back to your family?"

"Yes, I hope so. I said some terrible things to them while I was oppressed by foul spirits, and I want to make amends. But I'm going to tell everyone in Syria what Jesus did for me."

"Oh I hope you can be accepted," said John, "It's awful to be cut off from your family."

Nathanael broke in. "Hey, look at all the people gathering down in the street! I bet they're coming to ask for something from Jesus."

Sure enough, at sundown they began knocking at the gate. Jesus went out to the crowd along with Simon Peter and Simon the Zealot and Judas of Kerioth. Some of the callers were sick and wanted Jesus to heal them. Others brought family members they had been hiding in their houses, who were troubled by foul spirits.

Two of those cried out loudly, "Jesus of Nazareth, we know you! You are the Son of God!"

Jesus rebuked them just as loudly: "Be quiet! Say nothing! Come out, you foul spirits, and go away into the dry places of the desert!"

Jesus comforted the ones he had freed from foul spirits, and began laying hands on others with sickness or weakness or pains. The crowd kept him busy for hours and was crowding around him, begging him to stay in Capernaum and take care of their town.

Nathanael gathered up James Zebedee and Joseph Alpheus and Thomas, and the four of them came out to help restore order. They moved the crowd back away from Jesus and helped send the townspeople back to their homes.

It was four hours past sunset before Jesus had a chance to sit down, and his mother Mary served him an evening meal.[71]

33

THE EARS OF CHORAZIN

MONDAY, 30 JUNE AD 27, 4:00 AM

John felt a touch on his shoulder. It was Jesus, signaling for him to wake up. He got up and followed Jesus in silence out of the house. Yesterday Jesus had been teaching and healing from sunup to sundown. Today they climbed the low hills overlooking Capernaum under a moonless starlit sky, until Jesus found a small peak and stopped.

"John, wait here while I pray. And pray for the guidance of the will of the Father."

Jesus went 20 paces away to pray. John prayed as Jesus had instructed, but then he didn't know what else to pray for, so he watched the predawn sky as the dark slowly gave way to daylight.

As the sun rose, Jesus came to John and said, "We must go somewhere else, to the towns nearby. I must preach the kingdom of God to them also, for that is why I was sent." And they began walking back down into town.

John saw Peter and Andrew and Philip below them, and called out to them. When they got together, Peter said, "Everyone is looking for you, master. There are crowds again, coming for healing and to see your works, and begging for you to stay in Capernaum."

"Simon, I must preach the kingdom to the other cities also, for that is why I have come," Jesus said. "We will leave this morning."

Jesus and eight disciples got to Chorazin at noon, followed by a few men from Capernaum who had seen them leaving town. Jesus sent some 10 other disciples ahead of him to Bethsaida, his next stop, including Peter, Andrew, Philip, and James son of Zebedee.

Chorazin was a farming village in the rich soil northwest of the Sea of Galilee, and there was a small wooden synagogue. An elder of the village gave them access to the synagogue and some of the women in the village began to gather around Jesus, for they had heard about events in Capernaum. Most of the men were in the fields laboring. Besides the village huts, there were five large gated homes of those who managed farms for distant land owners.

One of the farm managers came down from his home to greet Jesus, and said, "Teacher, welcome to our village. I manage a farm for Nicodemus the land owner, and he has spoken well of you. How long will you be staying?"

"Until after the Sabbath," said Jesus. "I bring the good news of the kingdom of God,"

"Come stay at my house, for the synagogue and the farmers' huts are too small for you."

Many came from Capernaum to hear Jesus, but Jesus would not allow them into the synagogue until all the residents of Chorazin had found their way in. He preached the kingdom again, and healed many at Chorazin, and cast out foul spirits. But afterward, to John he seemed frustrated.

John asked, "What's wrong, Jesus?"

Jesus said, "These are like the people of Capernaum: they hunger and thirst for miraculous signs and healings, but they have no taste for repentance. Their ears hear me speak, but their hearts do not listen to the message of the kingdom."[72]

34

THE EARS OF BETHSAIDA

MONDAY, 7 JULY AD 27, 12:00 NOON

Walking east from Chorazin, they reached the shallow ford where the Jordan River flowed into the Sea of Galilee. Jesus was walking far behind, deep in thought. James and Philip were waiting for them on the other side of the river.

James called out, "Ahoy, John," and John answered back. After the disciples had crossed the river, James said, "Welcome to the land of Bethsaida of Galilee!"

Simon the Zealot asked, "How could this be called 'of Galilee,' since we just crossed over from the district of Galilee to the district of Trachonitis? Herod Antipas' territory is behind us, and we're in Philip *ben* Herod's territory now."

James said, "The Romans might have given the pearl of Bethsaida to Philip to decorate his rockpile of Trachonitis, but we know that we're the pearl of Galilee, not the pearl of a rockpile! This lake of Kinnereth of the ancients—the Sea of Galilee—was here long before the Romans, and it'll be here when they're long gone."

"Brother, I understand you completely," Simon said. "It's a travesty what the Romans are doing to the homelands of Israel."

"Yes," said James, "Herod Antipas is trying to change the lake's name to Tiberias, to honor the emperor. And Philip *ben* Herod is building playgrounds in Bethsaida to attract the Greeks, and trying to change the town's name to Julias, to honor the emperor's wife. But the fishing town of Bethsaida of Galilee will survive them all."

John asked, "How are mom and dad doing?"

"Just fine," James said, "They're looking forward to having you home for a few days. Dad and Jonah have been shopping for donkeys, and Jonah's sorry he had Andrew sell that donkey in Jerusalem. How long do you think we'll all be here?"

"Oh, I think a few days. Prob'ly till after Sabbath. Jesus wants to go preach in all Galilee."

The synagogue in Bethsaida was much larger than the one in Chorazin, and was built with stone instead of wood. Jesus preached there to a small crowd before Sabbath, and to a very large crowd on Sabbath morning. More people were brought to him with foul spirits to cast out, and Jesus was on the alert for them, telling them to keep quiet and not identify him as the Son of God.

Jesus kept on teaching of repentance, and of the coming of the kingdom. He told them "the axe is laid at the root of the tree," a warning that no one would be saved just because they were descendants of Abraham.

But Jesus said to John, "There are many ears in Bethsaida, but few that are not stopped up."[73]

35

End of the Tour

Tuesday, 30 September AD 27, 12:00 noon

John, Andrew, Philip, and Nathanael slumped down in the Alpheus house in Ephraim, glad to be off the road. They had been on tour for three months, following Jesus from synagogue to synagogue all over Galilee. From Bethsaida they had gone north to Sepph and Meroth, then southwest to Gischala, Ramah, and Jotapata.

From Jotapata they had gone west to Ptolemais on the Great Sea, at the ancient port of Acco. John and Andrew had seen the Great Sea for the first time, and they had enjoyed watching the grand sailing ships come and go. John had told Nathanael he wanted to see one of the mighty Roman warships. But Nathanael said, "Oh no you don't. If you see a Roman warship here, it means that war has come upon us."

From Ptolemais they had gone south to Besara, Yokneam, Afula, Jezreel, and finally Geraba. Crossing into Samaria, they had visited two days at Sychar, then arrived at the Alpheus house in Ephraim, where James and Joses' mother Mary greeted them.

Jesus had been preaching repentance and the good news of the coming kingdom of God at every stop, and even between stops. He had been healing every kind of disease, sickness and pain, along with paralytics and epileptics, and casting out foul spirits.

Large crowds had been following him, not only from Galilee, but also from Jerusalem and Judea. There were also people who had come from farther. Some had come from Syria, saying they had heard about Jesus from Jahath of Edrie. Others had come from Scythopolis, one of the Roman Ten Towns, which was near where John the Baptist had been preaching. And still more had come from the far side of the Jordan, saying they had heard about Jesus from Daniel, one of the Baptist's disciples.[74]

When they left Bethsaida there were 20 disciples following Jesus. Now there were 40.

Jesus was planning to rest and recover in Ephraim before going to Jerusalem for the Festival of Booths. In that festival Jews would live outdoors for a week in remembrance of the 40 years when Israel had lived in tents after they were freed from slavery in Egypt. The Alpheus family derived some of their income by renting tent fabric for the booths during the festival.

James Alpheus and his brother Joses were preparing to leave with Thaddeus to go to Jerusalem. The Day of Atonement was near, and both James and Joses were scheduled to serve as Levites in the temple. Within two hours they had loaded their donkeys and were ready to depart. Thaddeus said, "Goodbye, Grandma! Goodbye, John."

"Goodbye, Tad," said John. After they left, he asked Thaddeus' grandmother, "Mary, do you ever see Matthew, the tax collector?"

"Oh, not for many years," said Mary Alpheus. "He's the son of my husband's first wife, but I still love him. If I was going to ask Jesus for any healing at all, I would ask him to heal our family. I know his brothers miss him."

John said, "With everything else I've seen Jesus do, it wouldn't surprise me if he could heal families too. I'm going to ask him."

36

A Leper in Judea

SATURDAY, 11 OCTOBER AD 29, 8:00 AM

John and Thaddeus were hanging out with Hezekiah in the City of David, not far from Hezekiah's house. They had put up a booth with poles Hezekiah had scrounged up, and covered it with leftover fabric Thaddeus brought. All the Malchiel family was there, and Abigail was preparing a simple meal.

Jesus had been sleeping with them also, and the crowds had not been able to find him. They were looking for him, expecting that he would be among the rest of his disciples who were camped in the Lower City near the Essene Gate. But Jesus was wearing a cloak with a hood, and would come and go by night.

It wasn't dark yet, but Jesus appeared at the door of the booth. "John, I want you to come with me. I have been invited to teach at a house in Bethany."

Abigail asked, "Master, will you eat with us?"

"Yes, I'd be delighted to," said Jesus. "Thank you, I'm famished!"

Having slipped out of Jerusalem under cover of darkness, Jesus and John arrived at the house of Martha and Mary and their brother Lazarus in Bethany. These were friends who had met Jesus some years before when he had visited Jerusalem, and they wanted to hear what he had been doing and preaching. A few of their close friends were there also. Jesus reviewed the story of John the Baptist, and his call to preach repentance and the kingdom of God.

When Jesus and John left, there was a man standing outside the door in the dark. He asked, "Are you Jesus of Nazareth? I am Simon, called the Leper, a friend of Lazarus." John could see that his face and arms were disfigured by a skin disease.

"Yes I am," Jesus said. "What do you seek?"

Simon fell to his knees, and said, "Lord, if you are willing, you can make me clean."

Moved with compassion, Jesus reached out his hand and touched him. "I am willing," he said. "Be clean!" Immediately the skin disease left him, and his face and arms were clean and unspotted.

Jesus said, "See that you say nothing to anyone about this; but go, show yourself to the priest, and make the offering for your cleansing that Moses commanded, as a testimony to them of the power of God."

The man went off into the darkness, but later he told everyone what Jesus had done, and it became even more difficult for Jesus to enter a city publicly.[75]

37

HOLE IN THE ROOF

TUESDAY, 28 OCTOBER AD 27, 7:00 AM

Jesus was walking along the shore of the Sea of Galilee, followed by John, Peter, Andrew and Philip. The Bashan brothers were in a small boat coming to shore with a catch of a dozen fish. Jesus called out to them: "Beon! Bohan! I must teach in your house tonight!"

"Yes, teacher," said Beon. "We will tell our friends."

And their friends told their friend's friends, and their friends' friends told theirs, and before long everyone in town knew where Jesus was teaching that evening. First to arrive was a delegation of Pharisees and teachers of the law visiting from Jerusalem. They were in town because they had been invited by Jairus and the other rulers of the Capernaum synagogue to come listen to the things that this upstart Jesus of Nazareth was trying to teach.

The people continued to gather, standing in such large numbers that there was no room left inside, and the crowd outside the door spilled into the street. Jesus was sitting in a chair, with John standing next to him. The Pharisees and teachers of the law had grabbed all the other available chairs. Jesus taught them all from his deep knowledge of the Word of God written on the scrolls of Scripture.

Meanwhile a group of men arrived, trying to bring to Jesus a young paralyzed man, who was being carried on a pallet by four of the men. There was no way they could get him to Jesus because of the crowd, so they climbed the stairway to the roof and made an opening in the roof tiles. Using ropes, they lowered the mat the young man was lying on through the roof into the middle of the crowd, right in front of Jesus.

Jesus said, "What faith you have, men!" Then he turned to the paralyzed young man in front of him and said, "Son, your sins are forgiven you."

Some of the Pharisees and teachers of the law shifted uncomfortably in their seats. Jesus said to them, "Teachers, some of you are thinking to yourselves that this is blasphemy, and some are thinking that only God can forgive sins. Why are you thinking these things?

"Tell me, which word is easier to say to this paralyzed man: 'Your sins are forgiven,' or to say, 'Get up, take up your mat and walk'? But I want you to know that the *Ben Adam* has authority on earth to forgive sins."

So Jesus said to the man, "I tell you, get up, take up your mat and go home." He got up, took up his mat and walked out through the crowd, going home and praising God.

This astounded everyone. They were filled with awe and were praising God, saying, "We have never seen anything like this! We have seen amazing things today!" [76]

And Bohan said, "Yes, but who's going to fix the hole in my roof?"

38

THE CALL OF MATTHEW

Thursday, 30 October AD 27, 9:00 AM

Jesus was walking from Bethsaida toward Capernaum along with Peter, Andrew, Philip, Thomas, and the sons of Zebedee. By the side of the road was Matthew the Levite, son of Alpheus, sitting in his tax collector's booth, for the time had come when taxes were due.

Jesus said to him, "Matthew, son of Alpheus, follow me!" And Matthew immediately got up from his booth, left everything behind, and followed Jesus.

When they arrived at Peter's house, the grandson and the other sons of Alpheus were there, and they fell into one another's arms weeping with joy. Simon the Levite said, "Thaddeus, this is your uncle Matthew!" Joses said, "Matthew, it's so good to have you back with us!"

John watched all this and became weepy-eyed himself.

That afternoon Matthew and his wife Paula gave a big reception and feast for Jesus and his disciples, and invited their own friends to come also. A crowd of tax collectors and other agents of Herod's government, along with other well-known sinners, were reclining at the table with Jesus, and among them there were several who had begun following Jesus.

John met Matthew's five sons and one daughter, who ranged from four years old to John's age. The oldest was Matthew Junior, and the second oldest was Sarah, 12 years old. John had seen Matthew Junior going on his way to the advanced Hebrew language classes in the Capernaum synagogue.

Matthew son of Matthew was a very serious young man. He told John he wanted to be a scribe and a teacher of the law. They enjoyed each other's company and shared questions they each had about difficult passages of scripture. John invited his new friend to come over to Peter's house to look at the scroll of Daniel he was studying.

John was pleased to get together once more with all the disciples, for Jesus was releasing them to spend the winter with their families. He would not get to celebrate a holiday feast with most of them until next year.

After the reception, Jesus stayed behind at Matthew's house to talk with the Alpheus family, while John walked with the disciples to Peter's house. As they walked, they encountered Jairus, one of the rulers of the Capernaum synagogue.

Jairus approached Peter and said, "Simon, the visiting teachers of the law have learned that your teacher has been eating and drinking with tax collectors and sinners. They are asking, 'Why does he do that?'"

"I will take your question to him and bring you a reply," said Peter.

When Jesus heard this, he said, "It is not those who are healthy who need a physician, but those who are sick. I did not come to call the righteous, but to call sinners to repentance."[77]

39

WHAT, NO FASTING?

WEDNESDAY, 31 DECEMBER AD 27, 10:00 AM

John was walking to Peter's house just as Daniel and two other disciples of the Baptist emerged from the synagogue. "Daniel! Good to see you," John said. "How is your teacher? And what brings you to Capernaum?"

"Well, the Prophet is still locked up," Daniel said, "and Herod Antipas has not said what he's going to do with him. But everyone knows Herod's wife wants him dead.

"We've come to spend some time with you to fast and pray for the Prophet. We are fasting especially on this day, the Tenth of Tevet, when all Jews remember the time that the first temple in Jerusalem was lost to the people of Israel.[78]

"But Jairus, the synagogue officer, told us that the Pharisees have been complaining about you. They said the disciples of Jesus don't fast, but just go on eating and drinking. Is there a reason for this?"

John said, "I think I know why, but I'll take you to Jesus right now and let him answer your question himself. But what will happen if the Baptist is killed? Will his disciples just go back to their homes?"

"I don't think so, John. The Prophet has given us permission to join ourselves to Jesus' disciples, and that's what the three of us will probably do. But we can't just abandon him while his life is in danger.

"The other disciples are talking about forming a "Baptist" party, a lot like the parties of the Pharisees and the Sadducees and the Essenes. They want to travel the land to teach the principles the Prophet teaches, including showing fruits of repentance in their lives, such as sharing with those who have little. They say they know more than a hundred people who want to join the Baptist party."

"Well, I hope your teacher gets released," said John. "He doesn't deserve to die."

When Jesus heard their question and the complaint of the Pharisees and the teachers of the law, he said, "How can the guests of the bridegroom fast while the bridegroom is with them? They cannot, so long as they have him with them. The time will come when the bridegroom will be taken from them; and on that day they will fast."[79]

"Daniel, your teacher has been taken from you, so it is well that you fast and pray for him while he yet lives. A day will come when you will have other reasons to fast and pray."

Epilogue

....

The Son of God?

Wednesday, 31 December AD 27, 8:00 pm

John and Jesus were alone on the roof of Perpetua's house, relaxing under the bright winter stars.

"Teacher," John said, "I've been reading the scroll of Daniel the Prophet, and I think I've learned more about what you told me."

"Yes, John, tell me what you have learned," said Jesus.

John continued, but switched to speaking in Greek. "As you said, Teacher, Daniel has a vision in which he sees someone who looks like a "Son of Man," that is, a *bar enash* in Aramaic, who comes with the clouds of heaven.[80] This person is presented before the Throne of Flames and is given the kingdom forever over all people of all languages."

"Yes, John," Jesus said. "Whoever is near to the *bar enash* is near to the flames, but whoever is far from the *bar enash* is far from the kingdom."[81]

John thought about that, then continued: "Now this *bar enash* can only be the Anointed One, that is, the *Messiah* in Hebrew, who is given the kingdom and is named as the Son of God in the psalm of King David. This *Messiah* will save everyone who takes refuge in him." [82]

"You have correctly read this, John. And?"

"But Daniel also writes about another son. That one is a person who saves three friends of Daniel who have been thrown into a fiery furnace by King Nebuchadnezzar. The king sees him walking around in the furnace unharmed, and says he looks like a "son of the gods," or a *bar elahin* in Aramaic. [83]

"Now while Nebuchadnezzar believed there were many gods, we know there is only one God, so this king was mistaken in his interpretation of what he saw. The *bar elahin* that Nebuchadnezzar saw in the furnace must be the same person as the *bar enash* that Daniel saw in his vision.

So this *Bar Enash*—this Son of Man—would be a savior who has appeared before, and is the true Son of God, the Christ who we seek. This means that anyone who calls himself *the* Bar Enash will be accused of making himself equal with God, and people will try to stone him."

"Very good, John," said Jesus.

"But I am still confused. All Israel is longing for the day when the Christ, the Son of David, will be born and will walk among us and save us. But how can it be that this same Savior was walking among the friends of Daniel six hundred years ago? Has he done this before?"

"John, part of your answer lies in the book of the prophet Joshua. You are done for now with the scroll of Daniel. I will loan you the scroll of Joshua so you may learn from that also.

"And keep reading scripture, John, for Moses and the prophets write about me."

Notes and Suggested Bible Readings

1. Mark 3:17
2. John 18:15
3. A lepton is a Jewish coin worth four minutes of a laborer's daily wage
4. son of the law = bar Mitzvah in Aramaic
5. Luke 22:66
6. Actual inscription on a tablet found by archaeologists
7. Leviticus 5:7
8. Deuteronomy 6:4-9 NASB
9. Deuteronomy 18:15-19 NASB
10. Isaiah 51:14-16 NASB, cf. Dead Sea Scrolls Bible
11. Longer version from the Dead Sea Scrolls
12. Son of Tholmai=bar Tholmai in Aramaic=Bartholomew in Matthew 10:3, Mark 3:18, Luke 6:14, Acts 1:13.
13. Bethabara = place of the [river] crossing
14. Mark 1:4-6
15. Isaiah 40:3-5
16. Luke 3:16-17
17. Matthew 3:13-17
18. Genesis chapter 37
19. Psalm 143:2
20. Matthew 14:4
21. Matthew 3:7-10
22. Luke 3:10-14
23. Isaiah 45:23 NASB
24. Deuteronomy 33:6
25. Micah 7:14
26. John 1:19-28 NASB
27. cf. Isaiah 54:11-12
28. See David Flusser's article, "The Isaiah Pesher and the notion of Twelve Apostles in the Early Church." Translated from Hebrew in Judaism of the Second Temple Period, Volume 1: Qumran and

Apocalypticism (trans. A. Yadin; Eerdmans, 2007), pages 305-326.
[29] In Aramaic and Hebrew, spirit is a feminine noun.
[30] John 1:29-34 NASB
[31] John 1:35-42
[32] John 1:43-51
[33] John 2:1-11
[34] Luke 2:41-52
[35] Ecclesiastes 3:1
[36] Matthew 2:13-18
[37] Luke 4:1-13
[38] John 2:12
[39] peacock
[40] John 2:13
[41] Exodus 12:21-27, GNT
[42] Isaiah 53:7-9, GNT
[43] cf. Matthew 23:29-35
[44] John 2:13-21
[45] John 3:1-15
[46] Daniel 7:13
[47] Daniel 9:25
[48] Malachi 4:5
[49] Deuteronomy 18:15
[50] Luke 1:26-37
[51] Isaiah 42:19
[52] Isaiah 53:4-6, Dead Sea Scrolls
[53] John 3:22-24, John 4:2
[54] Son of Sabbas = bar Sabbas in Aramaic = Barsabbas in Acts 1:23, 15:22
[55] John 3:26-30 NASB
[56] Mark 6:17-20
[57] Pentecost
[58] Mark 1:14
[59] John 4:4-42
[60] Isaiah 9:1-2
[61] Isaiah 9:6-7 NASB
[62] Matthew 4:12-17
[63] Isaiah 61:1-2a
[64] Luke 4:16-30
[65] John 4:46-54
[66] Luke 5:1-10

[67] Mark 1:16-20
[68] Luke 4:31-37 NASB
[69] An ancient city in Syria, near today's Daraa
[70] Luke 4:38-39
[71] Luke 4:40-41
[72] Matthew 11:21
[73] Luke 10:13
[74] cf. Matthew 4:23-25
[75] Mark 1:40-45 NASB
[76] Mark 2:1-12
[77] Mark 2:14-17 NASB
[78] 2 Kings 25:8-9
[79] Matthew 9:14-15
[80] Daniel 7:13
[81] cf. Thomas 82
[82] Psalm 2:6,7,12
[83] Daniel 3:25

Thank you for taking the time to read *John and the Jesus Boat Episode One: AD 27, On the Road*. I hope you've been delighted by John as much as I was delighted to share him with you. *Episode One* is the first of a multi-part series that follows the life of the Apostle John through his appearances in the Bible and beyond.

Here is a sneak preview from *Episode Two: AD 28*.

"Stop, you thieves! Get out of my garden!"

John and Andrew were startled, and looked up from what they were doing.

It was just after sunset, the beginning of the Sabbath, and they had fallen behind Jesus and his disciples, who were walking far ahead. They had stopped to pick some cucumbers and small melons from the vines growing across the path. They had also been picking heads of grain from the edge of the grainfield, then rubbing them in their hands to shred off the chaff, and eating them, for they were hungry.

A small boy had been watching them, and then run off. Now the boy was back, along with two angry men. The boy picked up some stones and began to throw them at John and Andrew, and the men started to throw stones also.

"Run, John!" said Andrew, who took off with John right at his heels.

John and the Jesus Boat Episode Two: AD28, Woes and Comfort will soon be available for your enjoyment from Stonewall Press and online at Amazon. You're invited to "like" my Facebook page at Author Rolin Bruno for the latest info. Tell a friend!

www.ingramcontent.com/pod-product-compliance
Lightning Source LLC
Chambersburg PA
CBHW020139130526
44591CB00030B/142